The National Association of Expert Advisors™ presents:

THE ULTIMATE HOMEBUYER'S GUIDE

THE NATION'S LEADING EXPERT ADVISORS®

REVEAL THEIR

SECRETS

FOR BUYING RIGHT IN ANY

MARKET

Published by CelebrityPress®, Orlando, FL
A division of The Celebrity Branding Agency®

Celebrity Branding® is a registered trademark
Printed in the United States of America.

ISBN: 978-0-9857143-8-3
LCCN: 2012950221

This publication is designed to provide accurate and authoritative information with regard to the subject matter covered. It is sold with the understanding that the publisher is not engaged in rendering legal, accounting, or other professional advice. If legal advice or other expert assistance is required, the services of a competent professional should be sought. The opinions expressed by the authors in this book are not endorsed by CelebrityPress® and are the sole responsibility of the authors rendering the opinion.

Most CelebrityPress® titles are available at special quantity discounts for bulk purchases for sales promotions, premiums, fundraising, and educational use. Special versions or book excerpts can also be created to fit specific needs.

For more information, please write:
CelebrityPress®
520 N. Orlando Ave, #2
Winter Park, FL 32789
or call 1.877.261.4930

Visit us online at www.CelebrityPressPublishing.com

The National Association of Expert Advisors™ presents:

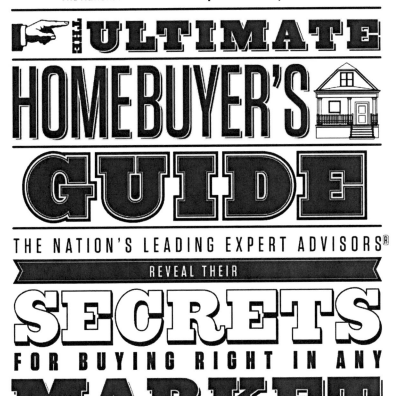

THE ULTIMATE HOMEBUYER'S GUIDE

THE NATION'S LEADING EXPERT ADVISORS®

REVEAL THEIR

SECRETS

FOR BUYING RIGHT IN ANY

MARKET

Contents

CHAPTER 1

Hire The Right Agent To Optimize Your Next Home Purchase

By Michael Reese

After my first decade of selling real estate, I realized that the biggest mistake new homeowners make is working with the wrong agent. So many new homeowners get ripped off and the bad part is that they never realize the true cost of picking the wrong agent.

There are many benefits that come with having a Certified Home Buying Advisor™ assist you on your next home purchase. As you start the process of buying your next home, be proactive on hiring the right agent with the right knowledge and experience.

You can do this by first making sure you look at your next home as an investment, with a goal of creating a detailed, comprehensive, Smart Home Buying Strategy™. Most prospective new and savvy homebuyers would agree that purchasing a home represents a large financial commitment, and that many key results of a home purchase could impact your future lifestyle in either a positive or negative way.

You want to find the best home on your terms! Having a strategy that approaches the process as an investment helps you control and manage The Home Equity Swing™ and produce the best results for you. My goal is to educate you with the key knowledge components you should consider when preparing your Smart Home Buying Strategy™.

The equity you create in your next home is what makes buying real estate a great investment over time. A lack of equity is what, most often, prevents homeowners from selling property when they would want to, and when the timing is right. Your equity in your next home will be elastic to many variables that you must consider and control. Many come into play before you have even picked out the home you want to buy.

So what is your future home's equity anyway?

The term home equity is the market value of a homeowner's unencumbered interest in their real property. That is, the difference between the fair market value and the outstanding balance of all liens on the property. Your property's equity increases as you, the debtor, make payments against the mortgage balance, and/or as the property value appreciates.

Homeowners acquire equity in their home from two sources. They purchase equity with their down payment and the principal portion of any payments they make against their mortgage. They also benefit from a gain in equity when the value of the property increases. Investors typically look to purchase properties that will grow in value. This causes the equity in the property to increase, providing a return on their investment when the property is sold.

This chapter is going to give you an introduction to the specialized "how to" knowledge you must learn and the mistakes you need to avoid – to help you maximize your next home purchase.

I. Overpaying for your next home is not only a preventable mistake, it is also one of the most common. Typically, it is never realized until it's too late or, even worse, never. Most homebuyers start their search online, and research shows that the home they end up purchasing is one that they found themselves. The problem with searching online is that every search site is not equal. The better sites using the best technology offer homebuyers more information to help determine the homes that best fit their interest. Unfortunately, not all sites show all the properties available for sale, or their current status, in real time. This could cause you to overlook the perfect house and not even know it was available.

It's a fact that good deals don't last long. The response time to notify you of price reductions, approved short sale listings, homes coming back on the market for various reasons, new listings, or even 'coming soon' listings, could have a very real impact on what you pay for your house and what someone with better information pays for theirs.

Emotional buyers love looking at homes, which can be a lot of fun in the beginning. Having a system, and a team, with specialized knowledge who knows on Monday morning or Sunday evening about a property that was just significantly reduced, could have a real part to play in the instant equity you create by buying a home under market value.

The biggest mistake most buyers will make is calling the sign to view a property where the agent not only represents the seller, but also has additional incentive for the buyer to buy that particular home. A well-trained negotiator will tell you that 80% of your ability to negotiate on a home is gone once an offer is written.

Negotiation is a very important part of the Smart Home Buying Strategy™. Having someone trained as an Expert, and who is looking out for your best interest, will help ensure you don't overpay for your next home. This mistake can be multiplied when dealing with new construction and the builder's sales rep whose compensation, bonuses, and promotion is all driven by the profit from their sales efforts.

Fact: The new homebuilder's sales rep's ability to be nice, polite, and listen to your needs is a function of their training. The more you pay for new construction, the more the sales representative makes. Don't be fooled – new construction benefits homebuyers when dealing with a local Expert Advisor™.

II. Overpaying for your loan is a mistake that should never happen. So what causes homebuyers to overpay for their home loan? And how do you prevent this from happening? Well, there are many things that cause this to happen. The most overlooked opportunity to prevent this from happening is getting a lender to give you a Good Faith Estimate before divulging your social security number and paying for a credit report.

A Good Faith Estimate is a form that lists the terms and all the costs of your home loan. Getting these fees discussed upfront even if the lender comes highly recommended from a friend or family member is always best practice. Being a comparison shopper will discourage most lenders from slipping in both inflated and junk fees.

A Smart Home Buying Strategy™ takes into account all of the fees associated with buying and owning a home. Since most homebuyers obtain financing, having someone knowledgeable about costs and the little things that could potentially lower your interest rate or make the most beneficial loan programs available, can have a very real impact. For example, optimizing your credit score is always a good practice and can directly impact your interest rate positively!

Understanding the variables that impact your loan and the cost associated with your loan are very important part of your Smart Home Buying Strategy™. Buying a great home can also, with the right strategy, translate into a great investment. Here are few things to consider that will help you win before you start:

III. One way to accelerate your equity and build wealth with your home purchase is to buy a home under the market value. Having a home search process that allows you to identify and segment certain seller types is the best place to start. Types of property or situations in which homesellers might be willing to sell below market are:

- Bank Owned
- Short Sales
- Distressed Sellers
- Divorced Couples
- DOM (Days On Market)
- Vacant Homes

There are also a few other variables that accelerate your equity over time associated with the home loan like:

- Buying down interest rates
- Local and National home buying incentives like grants and loan programs
- Mortgage Acceleration Program

There are many more. As the old saying goes, "An ounce of prevention is worth a pound of cure."

Preventing these mistakes is just one part of the process. If you really want to maximize this opportunity you can't stop once you have found the perfect home, and have the perfect loan. There are many opportunities that you have to consider to execute a Smart Home Buying Strategy™.

The home buying process can be very taxing. Don't put yourself in an emotionally-compromised position of just wanting to get it over and done with. This is usually the result of a poorly-constructed plan, or, no real plan in the first place. Understand that most homesellers are just as motivated to get the deal finished and closed. Savvy buyers recognize that this is an opportune time to *potentially get a seller to give you concessions sometimes totaling thousands of dollars more than you might expect.*

This can happen even after you have already negotiated a sales price. Having a great home inspector and an Expert Advisor™ who has specialized training in negotiations is the key to making this happen.

A Smart Home Buying Strategy™ will take all of these variables into consideration. Sure, today's real estate market might have some of the best deals in history, but how do you take advantage of it? It's simple! By having a Smart Home Buying Strategy™, you can make a smart investment in your next home.

You can learn the facts behind the Smart Home Buying Strategy™ by reading the free report titled: *7 Costly Mistakes Home Buyers are Making Today.* You can go online to download a free copy at: www.7HomeBuyerMistakes.com

This report also contains "The 12 Most Important Questions You Need To Ask Any Agent Before Putting Your Home on The Market." So make sure you win before you start by making sure you hire the right agent.

About Michael and Jay

Michael Reese

Jay Kinder

More than 10 years ago, Michael Reese and Jay Kinder inadvertently caught up with each other one summer afternoon at Lake Texoma. Real estate was the discussion of the day as a young Jay Kinder shared how he sold 233 homes the prior year to a very open-minded Michael Reese. Who knew that a chance encounter would turn into the wildly successful partnership that is now Kinder Reese Real Estate Partners?

Since that day, Michael, Jay and their teams have sold more than 4,250 homes combined. Together, they've brought in more than $18,000,000 in commissions for their real estate businesses and haven't looked back since that fateful day.

Both Jay and Mike have been members of REALTOR® Magazine's prestigious **"30 Under 30"** group. They have also both been ranked within the top 100 of the 400 most successful real estate teams in North America by Real Trends of *The Wall Street Journal.*

Individually, Jay has established himself as one of the top agents in the world, selling more than 3,000 homes during that period while capturing 14% market share in Lawton, Oklahoma. In 2007, Jay was named #2 in the World for Coldwell Banker, competing with over 120,000 realtors – being the youngest to ever obtain this achievement. The results don't stop there. In 2007, Jay was also ranked #1 in Oklahoma and #2 in the Southern Region that included over 1,700 realtors from 14 states. He has been recognized with the honor of #1 Sales Associate in Oklahoma in 2002-2010 before opening his new company, Jay Kinder Real Estate Experts in 2011.

Mike, too, has enjoyed immense success as one of Keller Williams' top 50 agents worldwide. He is regularly ranked as one of the top five teams in the Southwest Region for Keller Williams, and he and his team recently broke the record for buyer sales for the Keller Williams he works out of in Frisco, Texas – one of the largest Keller Williams franchises in the world. Mike earned $1,000,000 in GCI after only his 6th year in the business and he's never made less since then.

In 2004, Jay and Mike started Kinder Reese Real Estate Partners with the aim of helping success-minded agents like themselves create the business and lifestyle that virtually every real estate agent dreams about. Kinder Reese currently serves more than 23,000 agents across North America with its revolutionary business model and innovative business systems.

In 2011, they co-founded the National Association of Expert Advisors℠ (NAEA), which offers the most prestigious designations a real estate agent in today's market can have. The Certified Home Selling Advisor™ has been recognized as a highly-differentiated, proven, repeatable system to earn sellers up to 18% more than with the methods of average real estate agents. The NAEA's goal is to provide the highest level of education, training and business materials to agents who are truly serious about bringing the absolute best consumer experience to today's home sellers and buyers.

The Certified Home Selling Advisor™ designation is a four-part certification process that helps today's real estate agents learn what they need to truly distinguish themselves from their competition, and establish themselves as the true, number one choice for real estate consumers in their market place.

They are both best-selling authors on Amazon's top ten list of books for small businesses with their book *Trendsetters* and they can be seen on NBC, ABC, CBS, CNBC and other major networks as Expert Advisors™ on the new television show, *The New Masters of Real Estate.*

Currently, Jay lives in Lawton, Oklahoma and has two sons, Brayden and Karsen. Mike lives on Lake Texoma in Texas with his wife Stacey, and their son Cache.

CHAPTER 2

Smart Home Buyers Have a *Smart* Home Buying Strategy

By Jay Kinder

You are about to make the largest financial investment in your lifetime and there is a good chance you will be completely *ripped off* in the process.

I've spent the last 15 years of my life dedicated to helping buyers with their real estate purchases in or around Lawton, Oklahoma. Over the span of my career, I've co-authored three best-selling books, have been featured on nearly every major TV network, *The Wall Street Journal*, *USA Today*, and was also featured on the cover of several industry trade publications. This summer, Mike and I finished filming a documentary about the controversial real estate journey that led us to founding The National Association of Expert Advisors™ in 2011.

As of now, I've personally invested in and own 26 rental properties, participated in over 4,100 real estate purchases, and flipped 71 homes with four more somewhere in the process.

Prior to founding Jay Kinder Real Estate Experts, I had earned the # 2 Spot in the World with Coldwell Banker for buyer-controlled sales. My message to you comes from multiple levels of experience, and many personal and professional mistakes. When it comes to buying real estate, you cannot afford to "learn as you go," so my goal is to share a proven method with you to follow – so you can avoid the typical mistakes most homebuyers make.

Most of our clients come by way of personal referral and willingly agree to our way of doing business prior to being accepted as a client. That might come as a surprise, but Jay Kinder Real Estate Experts is the complete opposite of what you might find in a *typical* real estate brokerage.

The major franchises that regularly approach my company "pitch me" their business model based on a minimum of 100 to 250 real estate agents. That creates a real problem for me. I am only willing to employ 8-10 real estate agents. Yet, somehow my small office of highly trained Expert Advisors™ manages to outsell all but one company in town, and we are gaining on them.

This "new way" of doing business puts a spotlight on the fact that the real estate industry has blatantly ignored the requirements to become licensed real estate professionals and advise homebuyers on the largest investment they will make in their lifetime. This is under-serving Americans looking to have their piece of the "American Dream." My rebellious position on this subject has earned the support of many real estate professionals nationwide that share in our vision and national media attention for the National Association of Expert Advisors™ (NAEA).

Although the majority of real estate agents are not qualified to advise you on your home purchase, there are many joining NAEA and investing in the required training to become a Certified Home Buying Advisor™. They can expertly advise homebuyers like you to create a Smart Home Buying Strategy™, and show you how to avoid the most common mistakes that leave you feeling like you've been ripped-off.

Ripped-off is a strong statement. Let me clarify. My belief is that lack of knowledge and experience shouldn't shelter you from responsibility. Many of my so-called "colleagues" are going to take offense to what I am about to share with you. They should. I've even come up with an acronym for them, the AFA, or "Average Frustrated Agent." You will want to avoid them at ALL costs. Unless, of course, you enjoy mismanaged expectations, negotiating from a position of weakness, beating your head against the wall, and throwing your hard-earned money down the drain. Didn't think so.

Furthermore, my prediction is that the real estate industry and its one million plus real estate agents are about to experience a "Darwinian thinning of the herd." The travel agent, stockbroker, mortgage broker, attorneys, and most recently insurance agents, have all experienced "disruptive innovation" and the AFA's will be next. I'll explain why this is important to you in a moment.

First, let me share a fascinating fact with you as a potential homebuyer. Did you know that the average real estate agent only sells about six homes per year? Yep, the person that is responsible for assisting you in the largest investment of your life and managing over 80 different variables across the home buying process only sells one home every two months.

Let that sink in for a moment.

Working with an AFA can cost homebuyers tens of thousands of dollars across the home purchase, and years or even decades in reaching your financial goals. You owe it to your family and your future to make a good investment when you buy a home. You cannot just rely on your real estate agents' convincing tone of voice and friendly demeanor to do it all for you.

Who represents you in your home sale matters? In fact, hiring a Certified Home Buying Advisor™ is the first step in this process. For the focus of this chapter, we are going to cover how to determine your Home Buying Strategy™ to increase your odds of having a great home buying experience and avoiding the common mistakes most home buyers make. The scary thing is that these mistakes costs homebuyers tens of thousands across the home purchase, and years, sometimes decades, in reaching their financial goals, yet they *rarely* even learn that they've made them in the first place.

WHAT IS A HOME BUYING STRATEGY™?

Very rarely does a homebuyer make a purchase out of straight necessity. Yes, you may need a home, but your decision as to which home you buy rests squarely on your emotional hot buttons. It's important that you are excited about the home you are buying, but the results of your home purchase should reflect a strategy that puts you into the best position overall financially.

To accomplish this outcome, you will need a Smart Home Buying Strategy™. This strategy is a simple one that uncovers every detail of what you want and need in a home, helps you find a home you love, and then engineers a buying strategy that makes the most financial sense now and well into the future.

- **Equity Buyer vs. Emotional Buyer -** Teaches you how to have your cake and eat it too. Ensures that you absolutely love the home you buy while getting a home that offers you the best financial profile for your specific situation.

- **Buyer Profile -** Complete a thorough profiling of your needs, wants, and desires before previewing any homes. Get absolute clarity on what you are looking to accomplish. What are your needs and what are your wants?

- **Perfect Lifestyle Neighborhood Profile -** Knowing the difference between the standards of living and the quality of life when it comes to choosing where you want to live is critical. Although much of your focus should be on how this home builds wealth for you, your quality of life enhancement is a close second place.

- **Higher Quality of Life Home Profile -** Determine what your wants are. These are the quality of life benefits you would like to have. For example, a pool is a want, but probably not a need. Make a list of everything you would like to have but isn't absolutely necessary.

- **Out of Pocket/Financial Strategy -** Determine what you are willing and able to invest into the process. Your Certified Home Buying Advisor™ should assist you in determining the out-of-pocket expenses, how to determine if you should buy down points on your mortgage, the pros and cons of 15 vs. 30 year fixed mortgages, and how to structure your offer to put you in the best position based on your financial goals.

Having a clear understanding of what your long-term goals are with your investment in real estate will help you make the best decision in your home purchase. If you have not completed your own Home Buying Strategy, you can do so by visiting: jaykinder.com/buyerstrategy.

If you would like to read more about how to find an Expert Advisor™ in your area, you can go to: www.A.com for a complete list of Certified Home Buying Advisors™. If you have downloaded this chapter online, you will also find the complete report "How to Avoid the 7 Most Costly Mistakes Homebuyers Make" attached. If you are reading a hard copy of this book, you can download the full report at jaykinder.com/buyerreport or visit: www.NAEA.com.

Before you take the next step, remember a Smart Homebuyer has a Smart Home Buying Strategy™. Be sure to hire a Certified Home Buying Advisor™ and member of the National Association of Expert Advisors™.

Jay Kinder

Michael Reese

About Jay and Michael

More than 10 years ago, Jay Kinder and Michael Reese inadvertently caught up with each other one summer afternoon at Lake Texoma. Real estate was the discussion of the day as a young Jay Kinder shared how he sold 233 homes the prior year to a very open-minded Michael Reese. Who knew that a chance encounter would turn into the wildly successful partnership that is now Kinder Reese Real Estate Partners?

Since that day, Michael, Jay and their teams have sold more than 4,250 homes combined. Together, they've brought in more than $18,000,000 in commissions for their real estate businesses and haven't looked back since that fateful day.

Both Jay and Mike have been members of REALTOR® Magazine's prestigious **"30 Under 30"** group. They have also both been ranked within the top 100 of the 400 most successful real estate teams in North America by Real Trends of *The Wall Street Journal.*

Individually, Jay has established himself as one of the top agents in the world, selling more than 3,000 homes during that period while capturing 14% market share in Lawton, Oklahoma. In 2007, Jay was named #2 in the World for Coldwell Banker, competing with over 120,000 realtors – being the youngest to ever obtain this achievement. The results don't stop there. In 2007, Jay was also ranked #1 in Oklahoma and #2 in the Southern Region that included over 1,700 realtors from 14 states. He has been recognized with the honor of #1 Sales Associate in Oklahoma in 2002-2010 before opening his new company, Jay Kinder Real Estate Experts in 2011.

Mike, too, has enjoyed immense success as one of Keller Williams' top 50 agents worldwide. He is regularly ranked as one of the top five teams in the Southwest Region for Keller Williams, and he and his team recently broke the record for buyer sales for the Keller Williams he works out of in Frisco, Texas – one of the largest Keller Williams franchises in the world. Mike earned $1,000,000 in GCI after only his 6th year in the business and he's never made less since then.

In 2004, Jay and Mike started Kinder Reese Real Estate Partners with the aim of helping success-minded agents like themselves create the business and lifestyle that virtually every real estate agent dreams about. Kinder Reese currently serves more than 23,000 agents across North America with its revolutionary business model and innovative business systems.

In 2011, they co-founded the National Association of Expert Advisors[SM] (NAEA), which offers the most prestigious designations a real estate agent in today's market can have. The Certified Home Selling Advisor™ has been recognized as a highly-differentiated, proven, repeatable system to earn sellers up to 18% more than with the methods of average real estate agents. The NAEA's goal is to provide the highest level of education, training and business materials to agents who are truly serious about bringing the absolute best consumer experience to today's home sellers and buyers.

The Certified Home Selling Advisor™ designation is a four-part certification process that helps today's real estate agents learn what they need to truly distinguish themselves from their competition, and establish themselves as the true, number one choice for real estate consumers in their market place.

They are both best-selling authors on Amazon's top ten list of books for small businesses with their book *Trendsetters* and they can be seen on NBC, ABC, CBS, CNBC and other major networks as Expert Advisors™ on the new television show, *The New Masters of Real Estate.*

Currently, Jay lives in Lawton, Oklahoma and has two sons, Brayden and Karsen. Mike lives on Lake Texoma in Texas with his wife Stacey, and their son Cache.

CHAPTER 3

The Art Of The Deal!

By Bob Sokoler

Experience matters when it comes to selecting an agent to represent you as a buyer. Imagine going to a doctor for an operation and finding out you were their first patient. In this chapter, we'll review a number of scenarios that could happen to you and your agent during negotiations for a home. Use these as a guide to interview prospective agents. See how they would answer the questions compared to the answers you'll find in this chapter.

THE NUMBER ONE NEGOTIATING PROBLEM

The biggest problem I repeatedly see are agents letting their own personality get in the way of negotiating a deal. Louisville Master Builder Philip Hill is one of the luxury builders I work with on a regular basis. He says "It's amazing how an agent can become so aggressive fighting for a better price for their client and actually destroys any chance of getting a deal." Philip has been in the home construction business most of his life and says, "…being too aggressive is a real deal killer!" He's right, a good negotiator needs to know when and how to be aggressive and when to lay back. Throughout this chapter, I'll share some tips on how to be both aggressive and win at the same time!

THE BATTLE

I don't care what part of the country you're in, a seller wants to feel like they've been in a battle and won! That's fine as long as you - the buyer - feel like you've won the war. Unless you're in a multiple-offer situation (we will discuss multiple-offers later), never offer the listed price. It's just throwing money away. There's no clear-cut negotiating strategy that a good agent follows. Each negotiation is different, however there are some observations that an experienced buyer's agent can make by looking at the first volley between buyer and seller. An experienced agent will look at a number of pieces of data before suggesting an offer price to their buyer. The information includes:

1) the number of days on the market.

2) a market analysis of similar homes (i.e. comparables or "comps") that have sold in the subdivision and ZIP Code.

3) the original or most recent purchase price of the home you want to buy.

4) any improvements made to the home since it was purchased by the current owners.

5) any potential problems the home appears to have (for example, missing roof shingles, leaks in the basement, stained carpeting, 15-year-old HVAC system, dripping faucets and a host of other items).

6) what the property valuation administration (PVA) has appraised the property for (though this could easily be out of date).

7) the difference between list price and sales price of homes in that given neighborhood.

8) the motivation of the sellers to move (this can sometimes be difficult to find out from the seller's agent).

9) curb appeal compared to other homes on the block.

10) materials used in the construction of the home as compared to other homes on the block.

THE LOWBALL OFFER

I don't know of a single buyer who wishes they would've paid more for a home. It's human nature to try to get the best deal. Some buyers want more than a great deal, they want a steal. Part of that philosophy comes from listening to friends who brag that they got the steal of the century when they bought a house. You may find that the agent you're using will discourage you from making that lowball offer for a variety of reasons:

1) Making a lowball offer can shut down a seller. (Meaning the seller is so insulted they no longer want to negotiate with you). If that happens and you really want the house, it's possible you'll end up paying more for it than if you made a reasonable offer in the first place.

2) The seller paid a lot more for the house than the offer you're willing to make, so why would they even consider a lowball offer like yours?

3) "I know the agent for the seller, I couldn't possibly send them an offer that low. It would be embarrassing for me."

You need to ask your agent upfront (before you start seeing homes with him or her) how they feel about making a lowball offer. If your agent responds to you with one of the answers above and refuses to make a lowball offer, be prepared to find another agent.

AVOIDING THE SHUT DOWN

If your buyer's agent is worried about the seller shutting down and not responding to your offer at all (and yes, this actually happens quite a bit), you have several options. Have your agent call the seller's agent upfront. Explain that there's a problem finding value in comparables for the house. Have the agent explain that you are concerned about making a lowball offer and insulting the sellers. This actually is a great move strategically. By letting the seller's agent know in advance that you're concerned about insulting their feelings, you come across to the sellers as sympathetic and understanding. That may be far from the truth, but for negotiation purposes you want to put the sellers at ease. Any offer you subsequently make can then be blamed on market conditions, and not because you're trying to save money. In essence you want to look like the good guy, but can go for the jugular.

HAVE THE SELLERS DO THE WORK

As agents, we know that all too often a seller determines the price of their home by driving around the neighborhood, pulling up a sales price on their smart phone or looking at feature sheets. They actually make a decision on price based on looking at a home from the outside and comparing it to their home, using the current sales price (not the actual sold price) and arriving at the price at which they want to sell their home. It won't be until the seller actually starts seeing feedback from showings that the seller begins to realize their home is overpriced. In addition to calling the seller's agent and explaining your concern over insulting the sellers, ask them to come up with comparables that support their seller's price. By asking the seller's agent to check with the sellers and see if they know of any homes in the area that have sold and are comparable to their own and for what price, you're helping the seller engage in researching price. This strategy works really well.

PUTTING IT ALL TOGETHER

Here's a straightforward process for submitting a lowball offer:

A) Ask your agent to find comparable homes in a given neighborhood or ZIP Code that support your lowball price.

B) Send that information along with your offer to the seller's agent. Submitting those comparables with your offer should actually help the seller's agent go back to their seller and show documentation that their house may not be worth as much as the sellers think.

C) Add an additional note that you – the buyer – are concerned about paying for an appraisal that will show the exact information of your finding with comparables, that the home is overpriced

PSYCHOLOGICAL DESTRUCTION

There's another tactic that you can use when making a lowball that is so diabolical yet so low-key it will put you in a position of power, save you money, yet still allow you to come off like a nice person. It's a very subtle approach that will eat away at a seller, especially one that needs to or has to sell. It's all in the approach by your agent, and here's how it works. Very simply, very quietly and without much inflection in your agent's voice the following words need to be communicated to the seller's agent before writing out the contract. "How quickly can your seller get back to you with their response? The buyers have three homes on their list. This is the first one and we need to get them under contract in the next few days."

A typical response by the seller's agents will give us 12 hours or 24 hours, but what you've done is to essentially lay the groundwork that could really pay off. Let's examine that communication to the agent. We've told the agent – without making a big 'to do' about it – that you have three homes that you're considering, you need to purchase quickly, and you're basically not going to fool around waiting for offers to go back and forth. Psychologically you're allowing the agent for the seller to go back to the seller and let them know you're a *bona fide* buyer and not playing games. This strategy can backfire if the seller is not motivated or if the home is new on the market.

BEST? AND FINAL

Good agents will put an offer in that is commensurate with the data that we've described. What the seller does next is equally as important. For example, the house you're interested in is listed at $200,000, you put in an offer of $180,000, and the seller comes back with a counter of $190,000. Do you, as the buyer, accept the $190,000 price? Did the seller come down to their final price in this counter? Or is there more room to negotiate?

Remember the words "best and final." Those words usually indicate that one side or the other has reached their final bargaining position. I say the word "usually" because I believe there's still room to negotiate. In the example above, the seller has come down to $190,000. They did not use the words "best and final" so I suggest coming back at $185,000. Now the seller can come back at $190,000 with the words "best and final" or maybe the seller's agent uses the words "will split in half and meet you at $187,500." If you want to go for the jugular, you could come back at $186,000 and see if they'll bite.

That's exactly what happened to another builder I represent, Ed Devore, owner of MD Custom Homes. I remember negotiations over the conference room table with Ed and myself on one side of the table and another agent and his buyer on the other side. It was late and we had been at the table for hours. Ed had agreed to give the buyer an amazing deal on the house he wanted to build. The agent for the buyer knew that, yet he kept pushing. I could tell Ed had reached his bottom line. The other agent was unaware that he was about to kill the deal. During a break, I quietly went to the agent for the buyer and explained we were 30 seconds away from walking out. When the meeting reconvened, the buyer's side had a change of heart and the contract that sat on the table was accepted.

NEVER FALL IN LOVE WITH A HOME

Every once in a while we get a buyer who is so in love with the home, they have to have it and they'll pay anything to get it. It's one of the biggest mistakes you can make when looking for a home. The moment you let yourself become emotionally attached to a home, objectivity 'goes out the window.' I see it happen all the time, so we advise all of our buyers not to picture themselves in the home until we've gotten through inspections and appraisals.

THE SWEET HEART STRATEGY

It doesn't matter if you're going for a low offer, in a multiple-offer situation, or just trying to make a good deal, as my mom always said, "You'll get a lot farther with honey than vinegar." She's right! Oftentimes it's good to sweet talk the seller while going for the best deal. We highly recommend that a handwritten letter from the buyer communicating directly to the seller accompany the offer. This is acceptable and from my standpoint encouraged. Naturally, the seller loves their house and any improvements they've made to it. The letter the buyer writes needs to take that into account. First, compliment the seller on their taste and furnishings. Next, find one, two, or three reasons why you as the buyer have fallen in love with the house. Finally, express how you plan to take care of the home and preserve it in the future. By the way, don't ever suggest any changes you are going to make to the house, as you might kill the deal. The letter works great to break down the financial battle, and puts a face and a heart into the negotiations.

FULL PRICE?

If you want the home, there is nothing wrong with making a full-price offer, but my suggestion is if you're going to make a full price offer, add $100 to that full price. Additionally, streamline the offer by minimizing what you're asking for. For example, pay for a home warranty yourself rather than asking the seller to buy it. Don't ask for closing costs; maybe don't even ask for the refrigerator. Finally, have your agent call the other agent to get a handle on what the sellers want (we'll discuss that in detail next). In a multiple-offer situation, most agents only discuss with the buyer about paying full price. So by adding $100 to a full price offer and streamlining the offer itself, you're thinking out-of-the-box. Add the letter about how much you love the house, and you may just have successfully swayed the seller to pick your offer.

SWAYING THE CARDS IN YOUR FAVOR

It doesn't matter if you're in a multiple-offer situation, putting a lowball offer in on the house, or just making a normal offer, you can gain an advantage by knowing the needs of the seller in advance. Before you and your agent make an offer on a property, you need to discuss with your agent what your needs are. For example, is your apartment lease up at the end of next month or do you have to be in the house by a certain date? Once your agent understands your requirements, he/she can call the other agent and find out what the seller's requirements are. It's possible the seller may need 60 days before they can move out. If that's acceptable to you, you can include a closing date 60 days from the offer and possibly reduce your offer price. The seller may not be happy with the offer price but seeing that you are giving them the 60 days to close may be exactly what they need and so the deal goes through. It's also possible that the seller is going to be on vacation during a certain week.

Other questions you can have your agent ask the seller:

1) Is the refrigerator negotiable?

2) Is the washing machine and dryer negotiable?

3) If the house is already vacant, can you rent it prior to closing?

4) Can you take possession of a home on the same day that you close? (In many parts of the country, like Southern Indiana, it's typical for possession to be one to two weeks after a closing.)

Including these types of items in the offer shows that you're willing to work with the seller.

About Bob

When it comes to selling Louisville Homes, Bob Sokoler and his wife/business partner Norine [and the Medley Sokoler Team] are ranked as #1 for full service agents in volume - among the more than 3400 Greater Louisville Area Real Estate Agents. For more than 20 years, Bob was a TV Anchor and Reporter - winning several Emmy awards for his work. Traveling around the United States as a journalist, and known locally as a technology expert, Bob combines his love of real estate with technology and prides himself on being on call 24 hours a day.

Bob is also a licensed agent in Indiana. With a larger combined market to work with, he is able to help even more buyers and sellers with their real estate needs.

In addition to reporting and anchoring TV news reports, Bob has been buying and selling homes while moving around the country for almost 25 years. From Flint, Michigan to Salt Lake City, Utah to Baltimore, Maryland to Orlando, Florida to Atlanta, Georgia to finally Louisville, KY.

In addition to his Emmy awards and winning other awards for his reporting, Bob's hobbies include Computers, Photography, Home Repair and Gardening.

CHAPTER 4

How To Avoid A Permanent Financial Disaster In One Step

By John Bretthauer
(also known as Johnny B)

SO WHY AM I IN DANGER?

It's likely my family scare will help you and your family.

Doctors nearly killed two members of my family. I don't know if it was incompetence or lack of focus. Either way, without intervention, their mistakes would now be permanent: Both my beloved wife, Vicki, and my firstborn son, David, would now be buried.

I stress the permanence of this.

Two other doctors performed spectacular surgeries that saved the lives of my oldest son and my Mother. I am truly grateful.

Clearly the solution isn't to avoid the professional services of a competent physician. The solution is to choose your doctor carefully, because life and death will be decided by their competence and focus.

But your risk runs a lot deeper than you might realize. Your outcome also depends on your doctor's office staff, vendors, hospital, nurses, labs and other physicians. Your doctor better have both the personal knowledge and skill—and also the ability—to organize and effectively lead a surprisingly large virtual team. This requires competence and vigilance.

The doctor and his team have your life in *their* hands. And there are no do-overs.

THE UNVARNISHED TRUTH:

We all know that there are incompetent "professionals" in *every walk of life*.

The educational process weeds out many would-be doctors. A doctor must graduate from a 4-year college or university, then graduate from a 4-year medical school, and finally complete a residency (basically an apprenticeship).

However, to become a Real Estate Agent in California requires 135 hours of education, the ability to pass an exam and a background check. There is no required apprenticeship to become a real estate agent. Your agent will also need to develop a large competent virtual team of lenders, inspectors, repair people, assistants, transaction coordinators, escrow and title experts.

Make no mistake – this is cardiac surgery for your finances.

BUY VS. RENT

Don't get me wrong. Stepping out of the rental market and into homeownership means you start building your wealth instead of your landlord's. When you retire, the average family has the vast majority of their net worth encapsulated in the equity of their home. If you are a renter – all that potential wealth is now your landlord's bounty. He will be enjoying what could have been *your* nest egg for *his* retirement.

Renters have exactly ZERO equity in their home. And they have to endure the uncertainty of being forced to move because their landlord decides to sell, raise the rent or terminate their tenancy. These moves are costly and inconvenient.

The uncertainty, inconvenience, and lack of equity growth add up to a lot of minuses. The 800-pound gorilla in the room is Uncle Sam, because every single year he will dig deeper into your pocket when you rent. And next in line to dig even deeper is the State of California. In fact, many renters find that 25% to 33% of their house payment can be paid by the tax savings (for more details, see GoJohnnyB.com for an article on the benefits of home ownership).

Buying isn't always the best choice. But all you need to do is a little math to figure out if it is the right choice for you. The Buy vs. Rent Calculator on my website is a free tool that will help you make the best choice (GoJohnnyB.com).

Currently, the math for a typical Bay Area family shows that if you intend to live in the home for more than three years – you are often better off buying.

WHO IS THE FIRST TIME HOMEBUYER?

The average first-time homebuyer is 31 years old and will typically buy seven homes during their lifetime. Each transaction has a buy and a sell side. That means you will typically have 14 transactions during your life.

Here's the question: Which of the 14 is the most dangerous?

The answer is: every single one of them is life and death for your financial future.

Imagine that you have a rope suspended between two skyscrapers and you must walk across the rope. Which step is the most dangerous to miss?

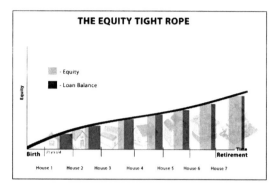

- Every single step on the rope could lead to a fatal fall.

- Every wrong real estate move can lead to a devastating financial fall.

This means that every single one of your fourteen transactions better be done right. This isn't a video game. You don't get three lives. And there is no safety net.

How do you get your loses back? Millions of people who have taken this fatal step have found out the hard way. You never get the money back.

SO WHAT IS THE RISK
TO A FIRST TIME HOMEBUYER?

Many agents are struggling to pay their desk fees, membership fees, MLS fees, and could lack the funds to provide high level services to their clients.

Many consumers assume their agent is full-time. The National Association of Realtors says that 30% of agents work between 20 and 39 hours per week. And 11% work less than 20 hours per week. Time is of the essence in real estate. Your transaction can go up in smoke before your agent gets off work from their day job.

Can buyers get in to see the property(s) as needed if your agent can't help until after he gets off work? And can the inspectors, appraisers, repair people, etc., get in as well? And what are the odds that a part-timer will be sharpening their skills, investing in technology and spending money marketing your home while working another job?

There is no legal requirement for a part-time agent to disclose that fact to their client.

THE GRAVITY OF THE SITUATION

When you buy your first home, you will typically make a down payment with the majority of your savings and spend approximately one-third of your income. Your house payment will typically take the lion's share of your income for decades to come.

One third here, one third there – and pretty soon it starts to add up.

SO HOW DO YOU FIND A GOOD AGENT?

All REALTORS® are licensed to sell real estate, but not all real estate agents are REALTORS®.

The term REALTOR® is applied to a real estate professional who is a member of the NATIONAL ASSOCIATION OF REALTORS® and must subscribe to the Code of Ethics which is strictly enforced. The Code of Ethics established a baseline of principles that come from the collective experiences of REALTORS®. Here are the primary principles:

- **Loyalty to clients** – A REALTOR® must put the interests of his client above his own.

- **Fiduciary duty to clients** – she must treat her client with the same care and concern as if she adopted her client into her immediate family. This is the highest standard of care under the law.

- **Cooperation with competitors** – Real Estate is confrontational in terms of negotiating price and terms of a transaction. But it is also a cooperative endeavor. It often requires more than one agent working together to complete the transaction. Done right, real estate is a confrontational/cooperative contact sport.

- **Truthfulness in statements and advertising.**

- **Non-interference with the clients of other agents who are in an exclusive relationship.**

RELATIVES, BUDDIES, NEIGHBORS, DAUGHTER OR SON OF A FRIEND – IN THREE WORDS – DON'T DO IT!

I made the biggest mistake of my life - long before I became an agent or really knew how much damage someone could do. I had already lined up a qualified licensed professional to handle our real estate. I didn't want to hire my relative. But I did so to preserve the "peace." He lacked the credentials to do the work but insisted that no one would take better care of *his* family than he would.

My wife knew him better than I and was instantly angry at me for trusting him. She is also angry at herself for not insisting on reversing my decision. It just *seemed* easier at that point to stay the course and hope for the best. Besides, how bad could it be?

I won't go into the details, but let me save you some grief and tell you what I learned and what I walked away with – and it wasn't the equity in our properties!

1) A seemingly sincere plea from a relative, insisting on *his right* to take care of his family, is not the equivalent to a demonstrated track record of excellence by a licensed professional.

2) When your directions are ignored – fire him anyway and cut your losses.

3) When you can't get your records – fire him immediately because the damage is now without measure.

4) It is hard to fire a relative.

5) Christmas dinners are really not fun – after sustaining a massive financial loss from a relative.

6) Losses on this scale can never be repaired.

7) It is hard to file charges with the Department of Real Estate and sue a family member.

GOOGLE YOUR AGENT

You would be surprised what you can learn about your agent.

Make sure your agent is web savvy. How good is your agent at promoting his own business? If he isn't very good at promoting himself, is he likely to be effective in promoting your home if you entrust him to sell it?

What feedback can you find about him? What do past clients have to say about him?

What credentials does he have?

Is he an active leader in his field? Is he an author, on the radio or on television?

It is always better to get third party feedback on your agent. One way to see an extended historical picture is to check out the recommendations found on LinkedIn. This long-term perspective will give you a much better picture.

Here is an actual example from LinkedIn:

"Johnny B is one of the most enthusiastic realtors I have ever had the pleasure to work with in my entire 35 year real estate career! He executes new ideas in a day or less, no procrastination in Johnny B. His visions and projects flat out impressed the heck out of me.

Johnny B is so positive and caring on everything he does. He is honest, bright, empathetic, creative and an absolute joy to work with. Johnny B helped develop projects with me and his contributions were nothing short of stunning!

Johnny B is a secret weapon to any business team and his "hard work ethic" is contagious. I am fortunate to be able to call or email Johnny and get his feedback or ask for his advice. He is always so responsive and his counsel has assisted me tremendously in my job as Vice President with Chicago Title in Pleasanton, CA. He totally understands the importance of confidentiality and I know I can trust him beyond reproach. It would be my privilege to recommend him to anyone!"

November 4, 2009, Ken Braillard, VP, *Chicago Title*

OLD SCHOOL OR NEW SCHOOL?

The answer is both. It is funny how many people are only gifted in one mode and are quite deficient in the other. Many New School agents are afraid to talk face to face or on the phone and prefer to hide behind their email. Many Old School agents just hope to retire before they have to learn how to use any new technology.

Old school methods are "tried and true." The most common failure of an agent is a lack of communication with:

- Other Agents

- Buyers

- Sellers

- Title Company

- Lenders

- Vendors

The essentials of the Old School methods include networking with other agents, having good negotiation skills and giving the perception to the agent community that he is competent to close the file. Old School skill is not: hiding behind a keyboard and being afraid to pick up a phone or go talk to someone to get the job done.

The New School methods are just as vital. About 90% of today's buyers will see their home first in photos on the Internet. Online marketing is not just posting a lousy photo on the MLS and calling it a day. There is a lot to creating visually-compelling marketing pieces that cause a prospect to focus on your home and to be strongly moved emotionally.

The people who lack the ability to create an emotionally compelling and pervasive online marketing campaign are quick to dismiss it as unimportant. That is ridiculous. Today the first impression is online. If you aren't there, you aren't seen. And if you are portrayed badly, at best you will have the market demand of a commodity.

But when the marketing is emotional, compelling and pervasive – you are maximizing the New School Marketing Impact.

Now assuming your agent understands all the New School electronic tools, can process offers at the speed of light and has the Old School skills as well – you've found a modern day warrior.

The good news is that there are many great agents out there.

The critical step in getting the outcome you want: you must choose your agent wisely.

THE BEST WAY TO PICK AN AGENT

No matter how much a consumer studies real estate and the process of choosing an agent, the agent you talk to has probably spent a bit longer in the field. And one of the things agents work very hard on is their presentation to *appear* competent. You need to ask yourself, will your BS detector allow you to spot the difference between someone who *appears* and sounds competent with someone who actually *is* competent?

The best-qualified person to tell you if your agent is a Qualified Professional who is committed to his clients and understands his profession is another highly-skilled agent.

I am painfully aware how much damage an incompetent person can bring into your life. I know firsthand that financial losses on this scale will impact you for life. People call me for help in picking their agent. I interview the agents and carefully choose a good match. The beauty is – there is no charge to you for this service. I don't bill you. I may have previously screened the agent from your area or I may have to make several calls to find the right person.

Full disclosure – the agent you end up working with will pay the small fee for this service. I do not offer a personal guarantee of their work, but I do screen them – and you end up with much higher odds of an excellent outcome.

So, whether you live in my area or not, you really should call me for help. Together we will help make sure your footing is sound in every single one of *your* 14 transactions on the way to your cozy retirement. Seriously, you should just call me.

RE/MAX Santa Clara Valley – DRE#01480256

About Johnny B

John Bretthauer (better known as Johnny B) didn't realize it, but his entire life has been building to his current position as team leader of the Johnny B Team at RE/MAX.

At age 13, he became an Eagle Scout. At age 15, he was awarded a work research grant by Buzz Aldrin (the second man to walk on the moon) to work at NASA. At age 17, he partnered with a NASA scientist and co-founded a technology company. Johnny's passion for technology became pillar one.

At 18, he attended a Kempo Karate school and was beaten black-and-blue on day one. His instructor said, "In the years I've taught, I've never seen anyone in such bad shape." Johnny became a black belt and studied in eight martial art schools of different styles, college wrestling and yoga. Johnny learned discipline and it became his second pillar.

In 1977, Johnny met Vicki, the love of his life and moved to Iowa – at that time a technology desert. He took a job as a door-to-door insurance salesman. He learned to listen, connect, build rapport, and develop discipline and persuasive skills. He broke the all-time national sales record for an individual. This brutal boot camp became pillar three.

In 1984 he founded a worldwide training company and published several books. His 204 presenters conducted trainings in Universities, hospitals, and all the branches of the military including local police and Special Forces. The marketing to develop 58,000 clients and the organizational and leadership skills became the fourth pillar.

Drawn to the financial potential in real estate, Johnny purchased numerous rental homes. He developed an investment strategy that has proven to be very profitable for himself and his clients. His fascination with the financial power and the proper use and danger of leverage became the fifth pillar.

In 2004, the world's number one best producing real estate agent of the 1980's, Jim Droz, agreed to mentor Johnny long before he became an agent. Johnny is a believer in world-class mentors and the power of standing on the shoulders of giants. This short cut to greatness, having world-class mentors, is the sixth pillar.

In 2005, Johnny B joined RE/MAX and began applying his six pillars and using his skills to help his clients get unfair advantages - legally and ethically. In 2008, he published a book to help families avoid foreclosure, "Wipe Out Your Debt With Bailout Money." Many people kept their homes through his efforts.

His Bay Area radio show, "Real Estate Rumble," was aired on KDOW and KNEW to provide the public with real estate information and protection.

He was interviewed on "America's Premier Experts" in Washington, DC by Emmy award-winning director and producer, Nick Nanton.

He holds the Graduate Realtor Institute (GRI) designation and HAFA Short Sale Certification. However, his favorite credentials are the referrals he receives from agents around the country, attorneys and most importantly, his raving fans - his past clients.

To schedule a no cost/no obligation, private Strategic Consultation for your customized Action Plan, call Johnny B at (408) 786-8904 or go to: GoJohnnyB.com.

RE/MAX Santa Clara Valley – DRE#01480256

CHAPTER 5

Save Time, Frustration And Money – With A Buyer's Consultation

By Doug Eastland

Does this conversation sound familiar?

Real Estate Agent: Hello, this is Mark Jones, how can I help you?

Buyer: Hi, I'm calling about the home at 2501 Village Oak. How much are you asking?

Agent: That home is listed for $229,000.

Buyer: That's great, when could I see it?

Agent: I can meet you there in about one hour, will that work?

Buyer: Yes, I'll see you there, thanks.

This is a fairly typical call to a real estate agent whose name is on the sign. Is there anything wrong with that call? Technically no, but in this scenario neither the agent nor the buyer are on the same page. The buyer is completely in the dark about important details of the home. The agent is unsure if this home is what the buyer is truly looking for, or can even afford.

49

Take a look at some unanswered questions this buyer may have about the home. How many bedrooms / baths does the home have? Will the seller accept this buyer's type of financing? Who is the agent representing? Are there any Homeowner Association dues? Has the home been updated? How does this price compare to other homes in the area? Are there other offers pending on this home? Are there other similarly priced homes we might want to preview? What about the resale value of homes in this neighborhood? And so on…

Now, look at some issues the agent didn't address by agreeing to meet in one hour. Did he ask the buyer if they were looking for a home in that price range? Is this the type of home the buyer is looking for? Has the buyer been pre-approved with a lender? Is the buyer working with another agent? How long has the buyer been looking for a home? Would the buyer like to see other available homes in the area? Where does the buyer live now and when are they planning to move?

Neither side wins in this scenario. The agent doesn't know at this point if he has a buyer or a professional home-looker. The buyer, on the other hand, may be wasting their time looking at a home that doesn't fit their needs.

Consider this: Would you ever use a Doctor who agreed to treat you over the phone without first meeting in their office? Will an Attorney agree to take your case before learning all he could about the situation? Can a Financial Planner properly invest your life savings without discovering your goals and risk tolerance? Of course not!

Why would a buyer want an agent to show a home and possibly represent them in the purchase, if neither side understands the needs and wants of the other?

The **most critical factor in a successful real estate transaction** is to have clarity about expectations in the buying process. Both the buyer and agent must discuss the details of the situation and answer necessary questions about each other.

Negotiating one of the most valuable assets in your life should be placed in the hands of someone you "hand" picked. How do you accomplish this? How can the buyer and the agent both start the home-buying process on the "same page"? It's very simple.

When a buyer starts the home-search process they should do a little research on "Top Producing" agents in their area. Do they know anyone with experience and knowledge of homes in the area they're considering? Have their friends had a great experience with an agent recently? People will gladly share their home buying or selling experience, so ask around.

Once an agent or two are selected, a ***Buyer's Consultation Meeting*** should be scheduled with those agents, in their agent's office. <u>This will be the most important conversation you'll have during the entire home-buying process.</u> Now is the time to address any concerns you have about the home-buying process. Here's your chance to ask questions **about** your agent directly **to** your agent.

Be open and honest about your wants and needs and share your fears and desires. This information is invaluable to a Professional Real Estate Agent. Your answers are how an agent decides what is in **your** best interest and how he can best help **you**.

What questions should a buyer ask at this first meeting? What questions should a buyer expect an agent to ask? There are no set questions or correct answers, but the following have been extremely successful for me and my clients. I'll ask the questions, first from the buyer's perspective then from an agent's point of view. I'll also explain why the questions are important and how they will help each side make proper and informed decisions.

QUESTIONS A BUYER MIGHT ASK A POTENTIAL AGENT DURING THE FIRST BUYER'S CONSULTATION MEETING.

- **Could you tell us about your background and experience?** How long have you been selling homes? How long have you lived in the area? How many buyers have you assisted in the last year? Do you offer any incentives to buyers you represent? — <u>You don't want to hear a sales pitch here.</u> Listen for answers that make you feel comfortable and confident in the agent's ability to help you.

- **Do you specialize in a specific type of real estate?** If you're going to purchase a particular type of home, you definitely want an agent with experience in that field. For example: if you're looking at homes with acreage, you certainly don't want an agent who specializes in condo sales. If you're looking at Luxury Homes, you want an agent that has current listings and past sales experience with higher-priced homes.

- **What times are you available to show homes?** If you'll only be available to look at homes after work or on weekends, make sure your agent understands. If they can't be reasonably accessible, what other options do they suggest?

- **Will you personally show us homes or will someone else be responsible?** Many and most highly successful agents have additional agents that work on their team. This isn't a problem; just make sure that your agent will be responsible for the final negotiations once a home has been chosen. Their experience will be critical at this point.

- **Do you have any testimonials we can see or past clients we can contact?** Any agent should be happy to share comments from several of their satisfied clients. Feel free to contact any or all they provide. However, be aware that these clients were handpicked by the agent. The simple fact that they have testimonials is a good sign.

- **Can you explain the home buying process to us?** No agent has the time to list every detail of a purchase transaction, but they should be able to explain the basic steps of the home-buying process and what a buyer will be responsible for. If something is unclear or needs further explanation, don't hesitate to ask for clarification.

- **How long do you think it will take to close on our home once we have an accepted contract?** Market areas differ, loan programs vary, contract terms and the seller's situation can all affect the days needed to close. This is another reason to discuss your situation and decide what is best for you. The agent will have a better gauge on the timeline once a home is selected and these areas are addressed.

- **Could you provide a list of vendors you personally use and recommend?** Here's where I often differ from what is taught to newer agents. Many agents will hand you a list of service providers and ask you to select whom you would like to use (i.e., Mortgage Lender, Home Inspector, Title Company…). A buyer selecting from a "list" of service providers is assumed to offer the agent and their brokerage less liability should something go wrong. I'm a huge believer in providing the names and recommendations of the vendors I feel will do the best job for their clients. An experienced and professional agent should know who the best service providers are in town. If their family asked who they should use, they wouldn't hand them a list! Choose an agent who is proud to put your best interest ahead of theirs?

- How much does it cost for you to represent us? A buyer's agent is paid a commission at closing, usually "by the home seller." Generally it costs nothing to have a professional real estate agent represent a buyer. You will more than likely be asked to sign a Buyer's Representation Agreement at some point, probably at this first meeting if you agree to let the agent represent you. This agreement defines the responsibility of the agent and will spell out who is responsible for paying your agent. Please read this document carefully and understand who is responsible.

Those are a few helpful questions you may want to ask a potential agent. There may be dozens more that are important to you. The bottom line is, always feel free to ask questions if they will help make an informed decision. If the agent seems hesitant to answer your questions or seems put out with the process…well, hmmm…move on. When the process starts out on the wrong foot, it will end up on the wrong leg for sure.

QUESTIONS A BUYER CAN EXPECT TO HEAR FROM AN AGENT DURING A BUYER CONSULTATION MEETING.

These questions help the agent understand how they can best help you make an informed home buying decision.

- **Will this be your first home purchase?** Why is this important? If you've purchased several homes and are fairly savvy on the process, the agent can focus on other areas. If this is your first home purchase, they will know to cover the smallest details to ease any concerns you may have about the process.

- **When would you like to be in your new home?** This gives the agent an idea of when to start looking at homes, how to structure an offer when a home is found, and time needed to clear up any issues. If you're not looking to move for a year or so, don't be surprised if the agent is reluctant to jump up and show you a list of homes. There's a good chance those homes will have sold by the time you're ready to buy.

- **What is important about that particular closing date?** When a buyer wants to be in their new home will show urgency on the buyer's side or will set target dates the contract needs to address.

- **Will there be anyone else involved in the buying decision?** Buyers will often want a family member to look at and "bless" their decision on a home. Many agents like to know this in advance for scheduling reasons. HINT: Most parents never think the home is worthy of their child and will offer their "opinion" on price and condition. Unless the family members are paying for the home, I suggest you leave the value and condition issue up to the professionals. Choose a home that makes "you" happy.

- **How long have you been looking for a home?** Again, if you're just now starting the search, your agent will have a good idea from your previous answers. If you tell them you've been looking for several years, don't be upset if the conversation comes to a halt. Agents are paid at closing and really don't have time to show homes if there's not a chance of payment in the near future. Successful agents are professionals and their time is valuable, so they're motivated to work with true buyers, not lookers.

- **How many homes have you previewed so far?** This begs the follow up question: did you see any homes you really liked? Are you represented by another agent (if you are, most agents will respectfully back off at this point)? Why didn't you make an offer on one of those homes? Was there a specific neighborhood where you really liked the homes? Be honest here, it's ok if you've already looked at homes.

- **Have you been pre-approved through a local mortgage lender?** If you're not paying cash, you'll need the help of a lender. Avoid the temptation, if possible, to use an online lender. I ALWAYS recommend my LOCAL lender. Trust me on this one; you'll save a lot of time, frustration, hassles and probably money in the long run. Get a second opinion, at a minimum, from a local lender. <u>You should be pre-approved through a local lender before you look at the first house!!!!!!</u>

- **What price range would you like to stay within?** Just because you're pre-approved for a million-dollar home doesn't mean you have to go that high. Stay within your comfort zone that will also allow you to enjoy your life outside the home.

- **What maximum monthly payment are you most comfortable paying?** You can base this number on what you are currently paying. If you are struggling with your current payments, your agent will know what price range of homes to stay below for your comfort. If there is excess income, your agent will know how high you can go according to your income. A good agent won't show you properties that you can't afford. <u>Another trust me statement: you will like the more expensive homes. Don't look at them; you'll set yourself up for disappointment if you drop down in price range.</u>

- **How much have you saved for a down payment?** <u>Your agent can estimate what your total monthly payment (PITI = Principal, Interest, Taxes, Insurance) will run based on the financed amount.</u> The financed amount is the sales price minus any down payment. Your down payment ability also tells your agent how to structure the offer and whether you'll need closing-cost assistance from the seller.

- **If we found the perfect home today, are you prepared to make an offer?** If not, why? What issues or concerns do they need to address for you to feel comfortable enough to make an offer? You'll never see all the homes on the market. If you feel it, do it, before someone else does. The properly priced homes in great condition don't last long.

- **What is your greatest concern about buying a home?** Price? Timing? Closing Costs? Updating? Repairs? Open up to your agent, they can help.

- Are there any questions you would like to ask before we move forward? Here's your chance to ask questions about issues that still concern you.

I know what you're thinking right about now. When can we talk about our dream home? When can we describe what we're looking for? When will you show us homes on your computer?

The answer is NOW. Congratulations and Good Luck.

About Doug

A native Houstonian, Doug Eastland has lived in Central Texas and called Waco home for the past 32 years. After a successful career as the owner of a sales and manufacturing company, Doug redirected his sales talents toward real estate 16 years ago. It wasn't long before Doug was at the top of his brokerage, where he earned 'top producing agent' status for many years. During that time, Doug received a number of awards, including *Realtor of the Year*, from his local board. He was the first agent in his area to implement the team concept in real estate, *The Eastland Group*. Doug is a Certified Home Selling Advisor and a member of the National Association of Expert Advisors.

Because of his proven track record and knack for growing businesses, a national Title Insurance Company recruited Doug to be their new Division President. Within the year, that firm grew to a solid #1 in market share, where it stayed during his entire term as President. Knowing he would someday return to real estate, Doug saw an opportunity. Teaming with a past *Eastland Group* member, the two were awarded a national real estate franchise for the Waco area, and then expanded into several surrounding markets.

Doug's passion and talent for helping other agents grow their business is the driving force behind his latest venture, *Eastland Systems*. This newly-launched real estate coaching and consulting company has Doug traveling around the country sharing his views on selling homes and assisting buyers. His no-nonsense approach to mastering the basics of real estate is drawing rave reviews from agents who attend his seminars.

Doug is currently the Manager of Magnolia Realty, a locally-owned brokerage serving the Central Texas market. Doug is a Certified New Home Specialist, Accredited Luxury Home Specialist, Negotiation Expert and Property Marketing Expert to name a few. He can be reached at: doug@eastlandsystems.com , www.sellingwacohomes.com or directly at: 254-722-4333.

CHAPTER 6

Dealing Effectively With Homebuilders

By Rodney Hamp & Jennifer Hamp

Choosing and dealing effectively with the right homebuilder can be a challenge. This chapter will guide you through the process of determining which homebuilder is best for you, how to negotiate the best deal and understand the maze associated with the process.

Most consumers make their decision of which builder to use based on the following:

- Floor Plan

- Location (neighborhood & schools)

- Model Home Decorations

- Sales Counselor (likes him/her)

- Perceived Value

Although they are factors, they are not legitimate reasons for choosing a builder. A builder's reputation, ethical business practices, problem solving, communication and employee turnover are vital factors. Researching complaints on the Internet can be helpful, however, it is not the number of complaints that are as important as the ratio of complaints to the number of homes they build. If a builder had 3 complaints in 1 year but built 25 homes, compared to another builder with 5 complaints with 900 homes built, the numbers speak for themselves.

1. DO I NEED A REALTOR?

Before you spend a lot of time searching for homebuilders, floor plans, communities, schools, etc., solidify in your mind if you need a professional Realtor to guide you through the process. As a previous Sales Consultant and Sales Manager for both local and national homebuilders, I can assure you that choosing a professional Realtor who is knowledgeable about builders and the construction process will save you a lot of time, money and reduce the stress related to the process.

Homebuilders spend an enormous amount of money catering to the Realtor community because approximately 90% of their sales come from Realtors. If a Realtor is a high-profile, top producer, builders are more likely to give the buyer as much as possible with the goal of developing a relationship. Many homebuilders have a "love-hate" relationship with the Realtor community. They embrace Realtors for the repeat business, but they are not aware of how much work has been done prior to walking through their doors.

Homebuilders view buyers as a one-time sale and view Realtors as a source of repeat business. The sales counselor's goal is to build a rapport with the Realtor. The Realtor always has more negotiating power than an individual buyer.

Just like in any profession, all Realtors are not created equal. When planning the purchase of your largest single investment, do some research first. Refrain from making your decision based on someone else's experience, or utilizing a "discount" Realtor because they are willing to rebate you a few thousand dollars in commission. An experienced Realtor will ultimately save you thousands of dollars in the end.

Check your local MLS for Realtors. Google the Realtors name plus "Client Experience Ratings" and interview at least two or more Realtors. Although they all might be qualified, the one you choose should be the one with whom you feel most comfortable. More importantly, it will reduce the potential stress associated with the home buying and building process.

In most states, buyers do NOT pay the Realtor a commission, the homebuilder does. Since homebuilders pay their commission, many buyers believe they will save money if they don't use a Realtor. Although this can be true in some cases, it's <u>not</u> the norm. Realtors commissions are already calculated into their margins. Reputable homebuilders will never alienate the Realtor community by reducing the price if the buyer doesn't use a Realtor. If you ask a builder if you <u>need</u> a Realtor, the answer will always be "no." Common sense would indicate otherwise. It would be like going to court and asking the attorney that represents the other side to represent you as well.

2. TYPES OF BUILDERS

There are three types of builders:

- Select Builders

- Custom Builders

- Production Builders

Select Builders
Select builders are low-volume builders who have a few floor plans from which to choose. They typically build 1-25 homes per year. The client can often make changes but are frequently limited to cosmetic changes only.

Custom Builders
Custom builders have an architect design a house specifically for you, or make some major modifications to an existing plan. Custom homes are one-of-a-kind and very unique but will

take longer to build due to the builder and subcontractors lack of familiarity with the plan and the detailed workmanship. A custom home can easily cost 2-5 times what a production home costs – since the home is customized and has higher risk & waste factors.

In general, custom builders will charge by either fixed cost, or cost-plus.

Fixed Costs: Buyer gives a set number or budget to the builder of what he wants to spend. The builder provides the buyer a number of selections for which items and materials will be installed.

Cost Plus: Buyer selections are very broad and based on the budget combined with the availability of materials. Buyer receives a copy of every invoice paid by the builder for building the home, including overhead. Then the builder adds his fee, i.e., 15%, 20%, etc.

Production Builders

The majority of homes built in the US are from production builders, such as D.R. Horton, Pulte, Lennar, NVR, KB Home, Hovnanian, Ryland, Beazer, Meritage, and many more.

Production builders have various floor plans to choose from as opposed to select or custom builders. Some high-end production builders who are in the luxury home market are also considered semi-custom builders since they will "customize" the home based on your choices.

With the number of production builders nationally, it is virtually impossible to make a statement that pertains to all builders. Those who have worked for homebuilders, and many homebuilders, consider themselves to fall into one of two categories: "construction driven" or "sales driven" homebuilders. Although both are focused on obtaining sales, their approach and management styles are vastly different which affects the buyers experience and process.

Production builders utilize superintendents who are responsible for the construction of a specific home. Although many builders have high standards for their superintendents, some do not. The quaility of the home is not only based on which builder built the home, but on who the superintendent was.

Most production builders have company-wide contracts for the foundation, AC, plumbing and electrical work. Builders rely on the Superintendents to do the remainder of the work and hire their own trades when it comes to framing, sheetrock, siding, trim, painting, etc. The quality of the home can be a direct reflection of the superintendent and their trades. When a Superintendent leaves and goes to work for another builder, he will typically take his trades/subcontractors with him.

I have experienced many times builders building a high-quality home in one community and one lacking in quality in another. This is usually a direct reflection of the superintendent and his/her trades. You should ALWAYS get the house inspected by a licensed professional home inspector.

There are three times to inspect the home:

- Foundation inspection – prior to the foundation being poured.

- Pre-Sheetrock Inspection – which will inspect the foundation, framing, plumbing and electrical. This is done before covering the walls with sheetrock.

- Completion – prior to closing.

If there is a code violation, the builder will always fix the problem. Other items on the inspection report could be left to interpretation of the building code or merely opinions of the inspector. When addressing those items with the superintendent, they should always indicate why they choose to do something a certain way.

Construction-Driven Homebuilders - (CDH)

My first new home Sales experience was with a large construction-driven company. In my first training class the Sales Manager said "the first word you need to learn when dealing with customers is NO." With construction-driven builders, streamlining the entire building process takes precedence over everything. Although streamlining keep costs down, in many cases it will hinder the clients need or desire to make adjustments or changes. In fact, structural changes beyond the standard options indicated on the floor plan, and cosmetic changes after writing the final contract, are prohibited.

All Production builders will have several floor plans with standard structural options per plan. The standard structural options will be shown on the floor plan or brochure hand out, such as covered patio, third car garage, additional bathrooms or bedrooms, media room, etc. Your ability to make structural changes beyond what is shown on the hand out material, such as extending the master bedroom, enlarging the covered patio, moving a wall are virtually impossible, especially if it entails altering the foundation and/or the roofline.

Construction-driven homebuilders are typically large homebuilders that employ Project Managers (PM's). PM's manage both the Construction and Sales division within their assigned communities. Most PM's start their career as a Construction Superintendant in charge of building the home from ground to its completion. The problem is PM's have never sold a home or dealt with clients through the critical stages of choosing the right lot, floor plan, selections, upgrades, financing, etc. They are not involved in the process until the home is ready to start construction, therefore many do not appreciate what it takes to get the buyer to this point. Not all, but many PM's have a tendency to treat their Sales Counselors as merely sales personnel and not professionals, causing a high turnover rate. Typically PM's that don't micromanage the Sales Counselors tend to attract and keep the best Sales Counselors.

Construction-driven homebuilders usually have two sales counselors in one model home. I feel this is not in the buyer's best interest because the Sales Counselor's main competition is not the other builders but becomes the Sales Counselor in the same office. Construction-driven homebuilders believe this creates competition as opposed to sales-driven homebuilders, who believe it brings division within the office. It's very rare that there is true cohesiveness within the office of construction-driven homebuilders.

For example, if you buy a home from Sales Counselor #1 and need assistance on their day off, you might end up with a Sales Counselor #2 – who is not overly concerned about your problem because they only get paid by helping their own clients. Although not impossible, it's rare that there is a beneficial working relationship.

Sales-Driven Homebuilders - (SDH)
Sales Driven Homebuilders are vastly different in their management styles and this ultimately affects how the Sales Counselor interacts with the Buyer and the Buyer's agent. Although my clients needs and desires are always first and foremost, I would prefer that my client and I work with a Sales-driven company.

Most SDH's view their Sales Counselors as the most important persons within the company. They realize the clients first impression of the Sales Counselor, combined with their knowledge (or lack thereof), will make or break the transaction – as Buyers want to work with someone they like and can trust.

Sales Driven Homebuilders have a tendency to attract the more skilled and professional Sales Counselors. Construction-driven builders have a tendency to hire Sales Counselors so they can train and manage them, or in most cases micro-manage them.

SDH's will rarely, if ever, have two Sales Counselors in the model home. Many SDH's believe this brings division within the model home and does not benefit the Buyer.

Sales Counselors for sales-driven homebuilders characteristically have more flexibility when it comes to making changes, as most construction-driven builders have a "take it" or "leave it" policy.

3. THE "INCENTIVE" MAZE

Builders have advertised incentives, such as $2k, $10k, $25K towards upgrades and/or closing costs. It is usually not mentioned initially, but most builder incentives are predicated on using their mortgage company and title company for closing. It is a RESPA Section 9 violation for a seller to require a specific title company as a condition of the sale. Builders get around this by paying for the OTP (Owners Title Policy) as part of the incentive; therefore they can require the seller to close at their approved title company.

Some builders will give you something on the front end (incentive) and make up for it on the back end. Example - $20,000 in "free upgrades" may only cost the builder $10,000 in hard money as each upgrade has a profit margin. If you are required to use their lender and title company, you may find yourself in a position where the lender charged a higher interest rate and more fees, and by that recoup their money.

Many production builders have "discretionary" money, which is additional money over and above the advertised incentives that the Sales Counselor can utilize, to make the deal happen. The chances of the buyer getting the discretionary money is minimal as builders incentivize their Sales Counselor by giving them a percentage of what is NOT given to the buyer. Companies I have worked for in the past gave 20%. If there was $10,000 in discretionary money, the Sales Counselor received an additional $2,000 for not giving any discretionary money to the client. Remember, if you have an experienced, high profile Realtor, the Sales Counselor will usually give up the discretionary money. Why? REPEAT BUSINESS.

4. NEGOTIATING

Of course everyone wants a good deal, but keep in mind a good deal does NOT mean financially only. If the home is in the right community, with the perfect floor plan, on the perfect lot and zoned to the best schools, paying a little more may in fact be a good deal, especially when it comes time to resell. Getting a good deal financially and not being able to sell it due to a floor plan that is not desirable is NOT a good deal in the end.

I fully understand staying within a budget. However, you do not want to come home from a hard day of work, pull into your driveway and say "I wish I would have…" because you saved $35 month on getting an item or feature that was not as desirable.

When negotiating with homebuilders to get the best deal, keep in mind every transaction is a case-by-case. There are typically three times when a builder is more likely to negotiate.

    a) Grand Openings

    b) Close-outs

    c) Completed Inventory

GRAND OPENINGS: When builders open a new community, they are more like to negotiate on the base price (not upgrades). Their goal is to get sticks in the air. Activity breeds more activity, which relates to sales and consequently they are more likely to increase their incentives.

Some builders like to place "SOLD" signs on lots that are not sold to create urgency or try to direct prospective buyers towards different lots.

Keep in mind there is an added risk to being one of the first in a community. There is no guarantee of what is going to be built around you. Developers have a plan and typically stick with the plan. However, the developer can alter that plan if the market changes or a situation arises. Remember also, if there are available lots around you, and you're building a home that is higher square footage, you may end up with several smaller square footage homes around you – which may affect your resale value.

CLOSE OUTS: Builders understand they are going to lower their margins when they exit a community and have a few homes left. They prefer not to spend money having someone in the model and the overhead associated with keeping the model open. They prefer to take less on the remaining homes and move on to the next community.

COMPLETED INVENTORY: Completed inventory is where you can get your best deal if you're focused on a new construction home. Normally production builders get individual construction loans on every home built. Paying the construction note is the costs of doing business. After the home has been completed it becomes the proverbial "black hole" financially. The builder's carrying costs each month continues, i.e. construction note, insurance, taxes, association dues and maintenance.

About Rodney and Jennifer

Rodney Hamp, CSP

Rodney has an extensive background and reputation in new home sales as a top Sales Counselor and Sales Manager for local and national homebuilders. Rodney has won numerous awards and accolades within the industry and teaches action-packed classes for new and seasoned Realtors on – *"How to Deal Effectively with Homebuilders."* He focused on all aspects of the process including effectively negotiating the best deal for their clients.

Rodney served on the Agent Leadership Council for Keller Williams Southwest, which is made up of top producers. This dynamic 'board of directors' is actively involved in the leadership decisions that make the office more productive and profitable – thus allowing them to tailor their strategies to thrive in all stages of the market.

Prior to his career in Real Estate, he founded a technology company that developed a web- based, electronic coupon infrastructure – which was later acquired by a public-traded company.

With the shift towards technology in how homes are bought and sold, Rodney's knowledge and experience in technology, combined with new homes sales, brings huge benefits for his clients. His personalized service combined with his state-of-the-art marketing approach, is the foundation of the Hamp Team's success.

Jennifer Hamp

Jennifer's family has been in the Real Estate industry for decades and she is well known within the community. She is considered one of Greater Houston's top real estate agents with numerous awards to her credit.

Jennifer's first year in the business earned her the coveted honor of being Keller Williams Southwest "Rookie of the Year" and she is consistently ranked among the top 2% of all agents nationally. Every year since the beginning of her career, she has more than quadrupled an average Realtor's production.

Jennifer was named "Five Star Real Estate Agent for 2011" by Texas Monthly Magazine, Texas's largest and most affluent magazine with more than 2.3 million readers monthly. A blue ribbon panel of real estate experts award this based on rigorous research of more than 116,000 recent home buyers, the readers of Texas Monthly, Mortgage Lenders, and Title Companies, in evaluating and identifying exceptional real estate agents in the Greater Houston Area.

Jennifer attributes her success to her experience, professionalism, knowledge and ability to negotiate effectively.

The Hamp Team

Integrity is their foundation with one basic principle "meeting their clients expectations is not acceptable, exceeding them is!"

Hamp Team is focused on setting a higher standard for the real estate industry and takes pride in the reputation they've earned. Phone calls are returned promptly, appointments are kept, fees are fair and the level of professionalism is high.

If you would like more information on the Hamp Team and how you can receive a free consultation, call (281) 937-9800 or email: info@HampTeam.com

CHAPTER 7

How To Build Your Real Estate Referral Business With Expert Offers

By Sarita Dua

Everyone would love to grow his or her business with referrals. A referral means that you did a job so superior that someone willingly gives your name to a friend, family member, or business associate, and recommends that you will do a great job. An amazing referral are those past clients that go *out of their way* to insist those in their sphere use you for real estate services. If you are not offering a service or product superior to others in your industry, you will not get the referrals you desire!

Every home sale begins with a great offer. No homebuyer or seller will be happy enough to give a referral if they feel they have left money on the table or been held over a barrel in the negotiation process. A win-win for the parties in a home sale are not just a vehicle for referrals, it is *the* vehicle for referral business. Whether you are buying or selling your own home, are a new agent looking to build your business or a seasoned real estate professional desiring to perfect your approach; contract negotiation is the fulcrum on which all else balances. Get the deal right, and everyone is happy!

You can break down a superior, win-win deal into the following six parts:

- Price
- Earnest Money
- Downpayment/Type of Loan
- Closing Date
- Inspection Period
- Miscellaneous/Other

In a strong sales contract, each of these parts works in concert with the other parts. For example, if a buyer finds the perfect home with a price tag $20,000 over budget, then the buyer will need to purchase the home for $20,000 less than the asking price. What might motivate the seller to accept an offer $20,000 less than asking? Suppose the seller's spouse transferred to another city for work and the family has been living apart. A buyer offering $20,000 less than the asking price who agrees to a shorter inspection period or who can close in less than 30 days might entice the seller to accept that offer or at least seriously consider it. You never know what a seller is willing to take unless you write a bonafide offer and present it to the seller for their consideration. To get a better understanding of the art of negotiating a contract that will win for all, let's look at each element individually.

A. PRICE

Everybody wants to know 'what percentage discount can I get off the price?' We do it with just about everything we purchase from cars to appliances to houses. Three factors influence a seller's willingness to consider an offer less than asking price: the home's market history, the seller's motivation, and the comparables in the neighborhood.

(i). **What is the home's history?** If the home just listed or the seller lowered the price on Friday and you are making an offer on Saturday, the seller may be less likely to accept a low offer. If the buyer really believes the home is worth $10,000 less than asking price, then it is advisable for the buyer to wait a while before making an offer. For example, a two-week wait will allow the market—in the form of few showings or no offers—to educate the seller that their price might be too high. In other words, if the seller's price is wrong, they just don't know it without some time to get educated by the market. Conversely, if the home has been on the market for 90+ days already, the seller may be ready for any offer.

(ii). **What is the seller's motivation?** Perhaps the seller has already purchased another home and cannot move until this home closes or the seller is at the risk of an impending foreclosure. Either of these scenarios might motivate a seller to accept less than the asking price for his home.

(iii). **Comparables?** Selling a home can involve emotional factors. Emotion makes negotiation difficult. Data diffuses emotion. When you give a seller the facts about what has sold in his area by presenting homes comparable in size, age, condition and location that have sold for less than his asking price, you increase your negotiating power without fueling the seller's emotions. With the right comparables, compiled by a professional, you might even plant some seeds of uncertainty with the seller regarding his own pricing. By using data, you don't offend a seller and you allow them to see the big picture.

B. EARNEST MONEY

An earnest money deposit demonstrates to the seller the buyer's earnestness or sincerity in going through with the purchase. This money is a lot like a security deposit for an apartment; however, the seller normally keeps the earnest money if the buyer does not close after the inspection period or any other contingencies are met. Every market operates with slightly different rules, but in

Oregon, the average earnest money deposit is 1-2% of the price of the home. Therefore, on a $250,000 house the buyer would normally offer about $2,500-$3,000 or more earnest money.

Earnest money can also indicate to the seller that the buyer recognizes and understands the seller's point of view. During the negotiating, a buyer's earnest money can level the playing field a little in his favor. For example, if the buyer offers $220,000 on a $250,000 house, even a motivated seller might be leary about pulling his home off the market when the buyer has only offered an average earnest money deposit. A more substantial earnest money deposit of $5,000 proves the buyer is serious and committed. In the event that multiple offers on the property are received, the offer with increased earnest money may improve a buyer's odds. Don't get me wrong. The price and what the seller nets are most important. But all these other factors can help craft a more compelling proposition for a seller's consideration.

C. DOWN PAYMENT/LOAN TYPE

At every step of the negotiation, you need to remember (or remind your client if you are a Realtor ®) that both sides want a win. Don't come to the table empty-handed and expect the seller to be eager to negotiate. In any market, a buyer who has pre-approval and who is working with an excellent loan officer will have the better standing at the deal table.

Know your financial situation and make yourself a stronger buyer. If you are transitioning from renting to buying and your usual rent is $1200 a month, start saving the difference between your current rent and the amount you anticipate your mortgage payment will be. These savings will become your down payment money in no time, and will help you determine if you are ready to take on the additional costs of owning versus renting.

Have a local, accessible loan officer get you pre-approved. You want the loan officer accessible, because you will need him or her to prepare a pre-approval letter to accompany your written offer that shows you qualify for the specific amount listed in the offer. You also want the listing agent to be able to call the loan officer with any questions while they are evaluating the offer with the seller.

Some loans close faster and with fewer hassles than others do. While an FHA loan will allow the buyer to put less money down, it carries with it a greater volume of loan documentation and stricter rules on the condition the property must be in, since the bank has greater potential for loss if the homebuyer walks away from his obligation. An anxious seller who needs to move quickly might view another loan with some skepticism. On the other hand, a conventional loan with a 20% or greater downpayment might close more quickly for several reasons.

Appraisers might spend less time investigating a property purchased with a conventional mortgage; some will even do a drive-by appraisal simply to ascertain that a home sits on the property. This is all a function of the loan-to-value ratio – appraisal scrutiny goes up as the loan-to-value ratio goes up. Fewer regulatory hoops for the bank and the buyer to jump through on a conventional loan can also hasten the closing and, as a bonus, do not carry PMI (private mortgage insurance) as FHA loans typically will. Bear in mind that sellers might be less willing to negotiate with a purchaser whose financing has a good chance of delay. In addition, jumbo loans—those with amounts greater than $417,000 financed—can take longest to close and may carry a higher interest rate.

D. CLOSING DATE

When does the seller want to close? Usually the seller will want to close as quickly as possible, but they may or may not need more time in the house ideally. A good buyer's agent might say to the listing agent "Tell me about your seller and what works best for them." No seller wants to hold his breath and lose 60 days of valuable market time for a deal to close. If you learn that the seller wants to stay in the home until school finishes in

June and closing will happen in April, a buyer willing to rent the property back to the seller until June, thus saving the seller the hassle of finding and moving to temporary housing, might be viewed as a Godsend. Remember, buyers, that 30-45 days are the best conditions to close for the seller and that a 30-day rate lock from the bank will usually get you a better interest rate than a 60-day rate lock will.

A buyer who needs a lower price might have greater advantage if he understands the seller's timeline and can offer the seller additional time in the home. Now both sides concede something and both "win." As the buyer's agent looking for referrals, think about how happy and willing to recommend you the buyer will be when you learn the seller's timeline and effortlessly negotiate the best contract.

A shorter closing period will be a moot point if the deal falls apart because of inspections.

E. INSPECTION

Every state is different, but there is an average of ten business days allowed for the inspection period. During this time, the earnest money sits in escrow and the seller removes his home from the market (marked pending) while the home is inspected on behalf of the buyer. Inspection creates stress for both parties of the contract! The seller might worry that costly issues will surface with the home and that as a result the buyer's interest or the entire deal could be compromised. The buyer could possibly terminate the deal if something does not check out.

Buyers beware! While it is uncommon, the seller could have back up offers and be waiting for you to jump ship so they can accept one of those higher-priced back up offers.

Negotiating a winning deal with the right sale price for the buyer could be more favorable for the seller if the inspection time were shortened, thus decreasing the likelihood of the deal disintegrating. Request a shorter inspection time as a bargaining tool to make your offer more attractive to the seller. If you know you will be offering a shorter inspection period, book your inspector before you write the offer! As the Realtor seeking referrals from satisfied clients, you can save them both time and money by scheduling the inspections as follows: General Inspection, Sewer Inspection, Radon Inspection and any other ancillary inspections thereafter.

Do not schedule all the inspections on the same day. The buyer pays for each inspection. Do the general inspection first, as the overall health of the property will tell you what other ancillary inspections are needed. In addition, if there are major issues with the home found during inspection, then the buyer will only have paid one fee. Your general inspection is essentially your "get out of jail almost-free card," the insurance policy for the offer, or the baseline checkup for your potential home. You are buying an existing home "as is." The seller is not required to fix anything in order to sell his home.

To negotiate well, should something turn up during the inspection, use guidelines of what anybody would ask to be repaired and make reasonable requests; these requests are usually safety or structure related. You will be more likely to get what you have asked for. Often times it is better for the buyer to ask for a cash allowance at closing to do the repairs themselves, than it is to compel the seller to do them prior to close. Your goal is not to lose the deal over little things – while at the same time have the buyers know exactly what they are buying. It is their true due diligence period to understand the property.

F. MISCELLANEOUS PERSONAL PROPERTY

Personal property is the category for items that do not normally convey with the home – that you are interested in retaining in the residence. You might love the refrigerator in the house because it is just the color, perfect for the kitchen, and what you would purchase for yourself, but deals can be killed over appliances.

Don't get into the position of negotiating too hard on personal items. You can ask but do not make them a deal-breaker. This is personal property—used personal property—that you can purchase on your own. Moreover, if you are making a low-ball offer on the home already, don't "steal" the house and then ask the seller to throw in the pool table, hot tub, and children's swingset!

If the sales flier mentions that, "the treadmill stays," you still need to request it in writing in the offer. The written contract trumps the advertising and marketing material. Be very specific. You might go so far as to specify the "stainless steel refrigerator with model #___" so that the seller cannot substitute that fridge they had in the garage. Again, never lose sight of the goal when negotiating. You want both parties to feel like they won, but as the buyer or buyer's agent, you do not want to lose the $400,000 home over a $400 refrigerator.

Whichever side of the table you will sit on at closing; remember that the road there will be smoothly paved if you negotiate a win-win scenario before you get there. Realtors trying to build referral-based businesses would do well to negotiate stellar contracts for their clients. There are four things about a property you cannot easily change—lot, location, layout, and natural light. You can change your business with expert deals that lead to referrals and a wealth of information your client cannot get elsewhere. While you practice the art of negotiating, collect a Rolodex of professionals to whom you can refer clients in need. Keep a list of 2-3 plumbers, electricians, roofing contractors, closet organizers, etc., ready for clients who ask. Continually update your list and remove those contractors who no longer are the best in their industry while adding new vendors who are. Each professional referral you offer to someone else keeps your client coming back to you for expert advice even when he is not in the market to buy or sell a home.

In the words of Harvey Robbins, U.S. business psychologist, "Place a higher priority on discovering what a win looks like for the other person" and you won't lose in your next real estate deal.

About Sarita

Sarita Dua is a top producing real estate agent in the Portland metro area. Sarita has built a name for herself in her local community by delivering outstanding customer service. Her business is based on referrals and repeat business, with over 85% of her business coming from referrals in 2012 to date. She is known for her negotiating skills and actively teaches courses in her office and mentors new agents.

With over nine years of real estate experience and an additional 14 years of experience in high-tech sales, marketing and business development, Sarita has excelled among the top ten percent of producers since her first year as a Realtor. Sarita also boasts a robust repertoire of designations and distinctions, including:

- Certified Residential Specialist (CRS),

- Graduate REALTOR® Institute (GRI) and

- Earth Advantage's Sustainability Training for Accredited Real Estate Professionals (S.T.A.R.),

…all of which translate to exceptional results for her clients.

Sarita is a Diamond-Platinum Member of the Portland Metropolitan Association of REALTORS® (PMAR) Masters Circle organization, and is the group's current President (2012).

Sarita holds an MBA from Boston University (Boston, Massachusetts) in Entrepreneurial Management and a Bachelors of Science from Kettering University (Flint, Michigan) in Electrical Engineering.

A resident of the Irvington neighborhood in Northeast Portland, Sarita's interests include travel, photography, NBA basketball, gadgets and walking. She loves spending time with her husband, Bhupesh, her daughter Sejal (13) and her son Rahul (11).

Sarita's passions include the Alzheimers Association and empowering girls to excel in math and science.

To learn more about Sarita Dua or to "ask Sarita" any questions about real estate, contact her at: sarita@asksarita.com or call her at (503) 522-0090.

www.AskSarita.com

For real estate questions big or small: askSarita.com!

CHAPTER 8

Five Keys To Hiring The Best Agent

By Joy Deevy

Imagine that you have won the lottery and now have $250,000 in hand that you must invest properly – so that you benefit from this lump sum for years to come. Knowing that this money must provide for at least a portion of your livelihood for the foreseeable future, would you invest it yourself and roll the dice, hoping that you come out on top or would you seek out the advice of a respected individual who is licensed and skilled in managing money to get you the best results?

To me, it's simple.

My guess is that you would choose the latter to give yourself the best chance at turning your investment into as much profit as you can. In the end, you'd pick someone – an expert – to help you with the entire process.

I believe other smart individuals like you agree with this premise, which makes it so hard for me to understand this one: when buying a home and making a similar $250,000 investment – or greater – in the place where they will live for five to seven years or more, many people throw caution to the wind and work with the first agent they meet, or worse, they go through the process themselves.

That doesn't make sense to me in light of the fact that most people would never be so cavalier with investing $250,000 cash.

In fact, it boggles the mind. And, if it baffles you, too, then you will find this chapter of the book very helpful to you in purchasing your next home.

What you don't know can hurt you (and your bank account).

Based upon a recent study, there's a very good chance that you'll use an agent when you buy your next home.

According to the 2011 Survey of Buyers and Sellers by the National Association of Realtors (NAR), 91% of people who bought a home used a real estate agent's website(s) to get information on homes in the area in which they were looking. From there, 87% of buyers worked directly with a real estate agent to go forward and purchase the home.

Based on this statistical data, almost 90% of the homes purchased in virtually every market across the United States are done so with the assistance of an agent.

Here's the kicker: 42% of the people surveyed after the transaction was complete were somewhere between Somewhat Satisfied to Very Dissatisfied with the home-buying process. That means that just fewer than one-half of the people who bought a home didn't enjoy some or all of the home-buying process.

Is that what you want to have to say after you've made one of the largest investments you'll ever make? ...that you were only "somewhat" satisfied or completely dissatisfied with the process? My bet is no.

You see, relying on a true real estate expert can mean the difference between keeping and losing as much as $10,000 when buying a home. And, as the value of the home you're buying goes up, so do the stakes and the potential losses.

Lose $10,000, you say? Unfortunately, yes, and potentially a whole lot more. You'll understand why as you read on.

It's not that all real estate agents aren't going to do a great job for you. In fact, there are scores of good, capable agents in every marketplace, including my own. It's just that there's a difference between an average agent and an expert, and that difference can mean thousands of dollars to you and your family.

YOUR 5 KEYS TO HIRING THE RIGHT AGENT

Buying a home doesn't have to be like touching a hot stove to see if it's hot – there's never a reason to get burned to know what to do (and more importantly what not to do), on your way to securing the home of your dreams.

Here are five key things you need to know when you pick the agent who is going to help you with the purchase of your next home – to ensure that you get the absolute best deal for you and your specific situation.

1. Personality is important
When you're going on a blind date, the last thing you want to hear from the person who set you up is that your faceless date-to-be has a good personality. It's virtually the kiss of death.

Conversely, when buying a home, you want your agent to have a good personality. More specifically, you want him/her to have the RIGHT personality.

Having the right personality means that your agent knows how to get along and work with a variety of personalities, including yours. Your agent will be dealing with several parties between the time you start working with them, including the seller, the seller's agent, your loan originator, home inspector, appraiser and insurance agent – in addition to other people along the way. An inability to work these relationships successfully can cause you delays, stress and cost you money in the end. This happens because the other people involved in your transaction aren't going to give you the best opportunities and deals on their products and services if your agent isn't easy to work with.

The right personality also means that your agent knows when to push and when to back off when getting you the best results in the variety of negotiations that you'll encounter along the way to the closing table. Being too pushy can turn the other parties off and make them not want to work with you any further. Being too submissive can mean that you spend more money and miss out on opportunities to really get a solid deal for yourself. It's a delicate balance that really needs to be maintained for you to have the best outcome when buying a home.

Lastly, the right personality means that your agent understands how peoples' personalities work and operate under the Platinum Rule. Where the Golden Rule says that you treat people the way you wanted to be treated, the Platinum Rule dictates that you treat people the way they want to be treated. In the end, knowing how the variety of personalities work will help the home-buying process go much more smoothly for you and keep everyone – especially you – a lot happier along the way.

As the old American idiom states, you attract more bees with honey than you do with vinegar. Hiring an agent with the skill to manage and work with a variety of people who have a diversity of personalities is going to make the entire buying process more fun and profitable for you in the end.

2. Communication is even more important

The historical data on communication between real estate agents and their clients is fairly well documented. What it states is this: on average, 72% of home buyers and sellers are DISSATISFIED with the communication between their agent and them. Remember, this data is gathered after the transaction is complete, so it's very telling about how poorly agents communicate information, details and vital data regarding a real estate transaction to their clients.

Knowing this, you need to ensure that the agent you hire to help you buy your next home is extremely responsive to your wants, needs and desires and has a plan to stay in touch with you during the entire process, including well after your closing has taken place.

Here are a few things to look for in securing a relationship with an agent who communicates well:

- Agents with a team – Agents that have a team of people helping them run their business are going to be able to provide you with a much higher level of service than single agents that do everything themselves. Imagine doing your job and everyone else's job where you work. How well would you be able to communicate with everyone if you were doing everything yourself? Not well, is the answer, and eventually your relationships with these people would suffer as well. Agents with a team often have two or more people that can communicate with you and answer your questions during the process to make sure you're comfortable with every step along the way.

- Agents with a plan – Hope, as they say, is not a plan. And while many agents say they will work hard for you and hope that things turn out "okay" for you, it's not good to hook your cart up to a wagon without a map to get you where you want to go. Agents who have a plan – a system – to take you from where you are now to getting the home of your dreams with the least amount of hassle in a time frame that's best for you and will do the best job for you. Included in their plan should be how they will communicate with you, how you will communicate with them, what steps you'll follow and in what order you'll follow them to get the best outcome and a well-defined process for how your transaction will be handled by the various parties involved. Anything short of that and you're not getting good value for your money or the communication you deserve for the biggest investment you'll likely make in your lifetime.

• Agents with vendor relationships – Two heads are better than one and three heads are better than two. More simply put, the more vendors (read: service providers not on the team) your agent has to help him/her with your transaction, the better off you'll be. Here's why: if your agent picks a loan originator, home inspector, title company and insurance agent – all crucial providers in your real estate transaction – that he/she doesn't have a solid relationship with, your agent may not have a good handle on how these people run their businesses. The consequence here is that important dates and milestones could be missed along the way due to poor communication between the parties, costing you thousands in rates, terms and even down payment money. Good agents have a team of vendors they work with that they can depend on to "deliver the goods" and maintain excellent communication with you along the way.

Lack of good communication can literally stop your real estate purchase dead in its tracks and easily relieve you of your hard-earned money. Picking the right agent helps you avoid this problem altogether.

3. Top level negotiation skills are crucial
In today's new real estate economy, you'll find that there are many agents out there who need your real estate transaction to close more than you do. Unfortunately, with the average agent selling only six to eight homes per year and making about $37,000 before taxes and business expenses, things can get tight for them.

And sometimes, when anyone who is negotiating on your behalf needs the income from your transaction badly, they don't always put your needs before theirs. The result can be something painful – like overpaying for the home you're buying – all the way to completely miserable, with you losing out on the purchase and potentially losing your deposit too.

There is no exaggeration in my statements…these things happen regularly in the world of real estate when you don't pick the right agent to help you with your purchase.

Your best bet is to find an agent who sells at least two homes per month and has been in the business for more than a year. In addition to that, you will want your agent to have formal negotiation training provided by a well-known negotiation coaching company. The best case scenario would be that your agent is a Certified Negotiation Expert (CNE) and has a designation proving that he/she has received rigorous negotiation training and has a certification proving a course was passed.

With a CNE, your agent will know when to push and when to ease up during negotiations. He/she will also know what concessions to make on your behalf to ensure that you get better, more beneficial results in your negotiation later on in the process. A properly-negotiated real estate transaction is worth thousands in your pocket, and days and weeks free from the stress and headaches that plague other buyers.

4. Honesty is the best policy

I believe with all my heart that real estate agents as a whole are very honest people. We have a tough job and that's why we have the opportunity to earn a nice fee for doing that job.

Unfortunately, sometimes agents have trouble delivering a tough message, even though their clients need to hear whatever the message is, in order to make a decision about what the next best step is for them. This resistance to giving the whole picture for fear of rejection, pain or even hurting their buyer's feelings, plays a large part in the statistic I discussed earlier about client dissatisfaction due to poor communication.

Again, the reality is that some agents just have a tough time telling you what you need to hear rather than what you want to hear – and that can cost you money.

So, when it comes to pick the agent you're going to work with, make sure they can deliver the news to you in a straight-forward, professional manner. You need to be clear on every option you have open to you when buying your home. So open, honest communication is what you should want and seek out from your agent.

Don't be afraid to quiz the agent(s) you're considering working with on their communication style, process and approach. It's like peeling off a Band-Aid: sometimes it's going to hurt, you can pull the Band-Aid off slowly and sustain lots of pain or you can pull it off quickly and endure a little more pain, only for a shorter period of time.

Make sure your agent communicates honestly and openly with you at every turn during your next home purchase. You (and your bank account) will be glad you did.

5. Market Knowledge is Key
In Latin, the term is scientia est potentia. In English, it means Knowledge is Power. The truth is, in any language, it's not the knowledge itself, but the use of that knowledge that is powerful.

Your agent should know your market inside and out. I'm not talking just about knowing what's sold in your marketplace, I'm talking about knowing all of the economic, employment, rental, sales, income, construction and bank lending trends that affect your specific marketplace.

There's a lot more that goes into determining which house you should buy and how much you should pay for it than what the comparable home sales were in the area. In fact, if your agent only uses comparable home sales to help you determine your home choice and offer price, there's a very good chance that you'll not be getting the best deal for your money.

You see, when we as agents look at the sales prices of homes in a specific area, we often don't know the "story behind the story" as to why a home sold for a certain price in a certain time frame. The home we're looking at may have sold at a lower price because of a divorce, the home smelled horribly, the seller wanted to get out from under the home quickly, the neighbor was a jerk, etc. These are all reasons a home would sell quickly and on the cheap that we would never know about unless we knew the situation specifically.

Not being privy to this kind of "inside information" however, doesn't keep an expert from doing his/her job. Your agent should produce a monthly market trends report that tracks several aspects of the data regarding home sales in your marketplace.

This report should be comprehensive enough to tell you how many homes are on the market in the various price ranges in your market, how many are under agreement, how many have sold, how many have expired, what the absorption rate is, at what percent of the listing price are they selling, and how many days have the homes been on the market.

By tracking and knowing this data on a consistent basis, a good agent will be able to help you pinpoint why homes are or are not selling in a specific price range and what it takes to get a good deal. Yes, an expert will know about the comparables in his/her market, but he/she will go deeper and farther than most agents in the same market to ensure that no stone is left unturned to get you the best deal.

Now that you know what to look for, finding the best agent for your needs shouldn't be hard to accomplish. Here's another statistic from the 2011 NAR Report that you'll want to take note of when seeking out the agent who helps you buy your next home. Fewer than 9% of the people who used a real estate agent to purchase a home interviewed no more than one agent before making a purchase.

If the first agent you meet stands up to your criteria – which are hopefully the same as the five I just reviewed with you – then by all means, work with that agent. However, if you have even the slightest doubt in your mind, you owe it to yourself to meet with another agent or two before you make your decision.

No two agents are alike and you deserve the best one when you're making a HUGE purchase for your family and yourself. Take the time to find the right agent and you should be in great hands.

About Joy

Joy Deevy is an experienced real estate agent and has earned the #1 individual real estate agent ranking in home sales for Coldwell Banker of Alexandria from 2006 through 2011. With over ten years of experience in the real estate industry, Joy is a Certified Negotiation Expert (CNE) and has her Certified Home Selling Advisor (CHSA) designation from the National Association of Expert Advisors.

She is also among the top 1% of Coldwell Banker agents in the entire nation. Joy has sold over 400 homes and more than $200 million in residential real estate in her career.

Joy currently lives in Northern Virginia with her husband Tom and their two children.

CHAPTER 9

Five Strategies To Follow At Least 6 Months Before You Buy A Home
— That Can Save You Thousands, and Lots of Sleepless Nights!

By Diane Cardano-Casacio

John and Susie had their second child about one year ago. As you can imagine the space was getting limited in their townhome. They really wanted to move into a single family home that offered larger rooms, a place to store the kids toys, a man cave for John and a place for Susie to work from home. The challenge they faced was how to sell their current home, take that equity and purchase a new home all at the same time. They were concerned that they may sell their home too quickly and rush into buying just any home, not their dream home. They also they felt anxious that they might find their dream home before their current home was under agreement. They felt that the Seller might not consider their offer – especially if there was another buyer interested who did not have a home sale contingency.

We call John and Susie the average "Move Up" buyer. Every "Move Up" buyer has the same concern. The first questions they ask are, "How do we do buy and sell a home at the same time? What do we do first? When should we put our home on the market? Should we start looking for homes before our home is sold? Or should we wait until we have an offer before looking for home?"

In this chapter, you will learn exactly what you need to do to purchase your next home, when you should do it, who you should hire to handle your asset, and what tools you have available to you to maximize your profit when selling and buying a home at the same time. Your home can be one of your largest financial assets you will have in your financial portfolio. Therefore, you want to make sure that right now you understand the "Top 5 Strategies" you must put in place at least 6 months before you start the real estate process for a profitable and stress-free experience. We found a direct correlation between the amount of time a client comes to us to discuss their real estate goals and their success in the real estate process. If you wait too long, you will lose every opportunity to maximize your profit and create that stress-free experience.

Let's me take you through the John and Susie's journey to their new home purchase. They are the perfect clients who were coachable and understood the value of preparation.

STRATEGY #1: MEET WITH AN EXPERT ADVISOR

John and Susie were referred by a client who had bought and sold a home from us last year. Susie was searching the Internet and found several homes for sale that she wanted to see that were located in four different towns. She called into the office to preview homes for sale on Saturday morning. I explained the benefit of meeting for a consultation first prior to looking at homes. Further, I mentioned that looking at homes they may not be able to afford, or homes that do not fit their search criteria would not be a good use of their time. All this would do is add stress to the process. Just from the first few minutes of our conversation, I knew they needed my help. They needed direction, a custom home buying strategy and someone to create a profitable real estate transaction for them.

The first step is to find an expert who has a system in place that starts with the client coming into the office to review their goals and visions. Start with a private consultation with your Realtor® to understand your needs.

How to Find an Expert Realtor

1. An Expert Realtor® can be found leading a Team of real estate professionals. In many cases, an Expert has their own company and is not necessarily a part of a franchise real estate company. They have proven systems built into the home buying and selling process that produce bankable results for their clients.

2. An Expert Realtor® can be found by first interviewing several agents on the phone asking them the same questions. Go to my website, www. CustomHomeBuyingStrategy.com for a complete list of *"Questions To Ask a Realtor® Before Hiring Them"* and a copy of the *"Profile of an Expert Realtor®"*. Once you get the answers that are in alignment with an Expert, meet them at their office.

3. An Expert will want to design a Custom Home Buying Strategy for you before they sell you a home. They will not meet you at a property, hoping to sell you something. They are looking to create clients for life. Therefore, they will invite you into their office for a consultation to make sure you are the right client for their consulting services and they are the right consultant for you.

STRATEGY #2: DESIGN YOUR CUSTOM HOME BUYING STRATEGY

John and Susie came into the office with their children, excited to start the process. We showed them a video about our Team. First I explained how we worked. Then I started designing their custom home buying strategy. The first question I asked was, "What is important to you about buying a home?" And then, "Why is that important to you?" I asked John first. I dug very deep and found out that he really needed a "man cave." He has a demanding job and needed a place to unwind. This "man cave" would help him relieve his stress so he could be a better father for his children. Then it was Susie's turn. She needed to be within 15 minutes of her job. She earned the same amount of money as John. It was very important to maximize her work time as they needed the money to support their lifestyle. Being closer to her job would allow her to spend more quality time with the family. They both wanted a yard to entertain. They were both one of six children, and when the families got together, they needed space to play sports and run around.

After determining their needs, we searched for homes for sale on the computer that fit their criteria. I ran a cost analysis estimate for the new home. Our next step was to talk to a mortgage consultant about their mortgage options to purchase a home that fit their needs. At the same time, we needed to determine the value of their current home using our pinpoint pricing strategy.

As you can see, the first step was not to spend Saturday morning with John and Susie looking at houses. I had to first understand their needs and then decide on our next steps based on that strategy. We spent a couple hours getting to know their needs. Most importantly, we started to customize their plan to successfully move out of the small townhome and into a bigger home.

STRATEGY #3: REVIEW YOUR FINANCIALS & DETERMINE YOUR OPTIONS

John and Susie met with one of our lender partners who would help them fulfill their home buying vision. They had great income. John had excellent credit but Susie had to get her credit score up from 650 to 700 in order for them to get the best interest rate and lower PMI. Also, they needed to net $25,000 from the sale of their home and save $8,000 to $10,000.

Susie worked with the mortgage company to get her credit score up. She had to pay off a couple small loans then wait 30 days. They also needed to save money to get up enough cash to purchase the new home and still have some money left over to spend on the new house.

The mortgage program they were approved for gave John and Susie the option to ask for a "Seller's Assist." However I did not want them to rely on it. If we could get an $8,000 "Seller's Assist," then we would not need to save as much money. Also we could be a little more flexible if they did not net $25,000 on the sale of their home. At the current rate of 4%, if they asked for an $8,000 assist, their mortgage payment would only go up about $32 per month. This is a small price to pay for the ability to be flexible and room to negotiate.

Tip: A "Seller's Assist" is the process in which you increase the agreed upon sale price to an allowable amount by the mortgage company. This amount varies between 3 and 6% depending on what type of mortgage you choose, FHA/VA or Conventional. The extra money in your pocket at settlement helps tremendously.

Here are two scenarios explaining the "Seller's Assist" option:

1. A home is priced at $250,000, priced well, totally updated and it is in high demand. If you ask for an $8,000 "Seller's Assist", you could lose your chances of purchasing the home. The Seller may not want to work with a buyer who has to increase the sale price

as the home may not appraise for the elevated price. In this case, you may not be able to use the "Seller's Assist" option.

2. A home is priced at $265,000 in a neighborhood where other homes are priced $260,000 to $280,000. This home needed some work and has a smaller backyard than the others however, but big enough for your needs. It has been on the market for 90 days. In this example, the home's value could be higher and the "Seller's Assist" a great option.

STRATEGY #4: SELL THE HOME FIRST, OR BUY A HOME

Before you start preparing your home for sale, sit down with your Expert Realtor to analyze the possibility of you finding your dream home. How do you do that? When John and Susie came into my office for the first time, we looked at homes currently for sale that matched their search criteria. We also looked at homes that **sold** 6 months to 1 year ago. I wanted to make sure their perfect home was available now or had been in the past year.

Luckily for them, they found several homes that could meet their criteria. We just had one more piece of the puzzle to put together. What was the value of their home? At the consultation, I took them through my home valuation process. I had asked them to take pictures of their home and bring them into the office. I also saw pictures on the MLS from when they bought their home seven years ago. Using that information, I determined that they had the $25,000 in equity they needed. However, they had some work to do on the home to prepare the home for sale.

They attended one of my monthly Seller Seminars to learn about the home-selling process. We previewed their home to put together their specific strategic home-selling strategy. Then we determined a sale price based on the final product. We got their home pre-inspected to eliminate any potential deal killers and made some repairs. They also painted three rooms, removed all the clutter from the home into storage, and fixed the front sidewalk. They were ready to go.

Tip: Make sure when buying a new home you understand the availability of homes that match your ultimate dream home. If nothing is or ever has been available that fits your needs, maybe you need to stay in your current home, build some equity and save money for a year. If homes are available, prepare your home for sale and start looking for your dream home.

STRATEGY #5: - HOME SEARCH PROCESS

I reviewed with John and Susie some tips on how to maximize the home search process. Here are some of the tips:

(1) **Check your email daily** for new listings or price-reduced listings into your price range. Do not rely on searching for homes online, the list of homes emailed to you from the Realtor MLS has all the available homes for sale.

(2) **Try to do a "Drive By."** If you do not like the neighborhood, then you do not usually want to go inside the home. Also, you can talk to neighbors and get a feel of the area.

(3) **Use a small notebook** as a journal for your home-buying. The notebook will be for you to write down notes through your journey of finding a home. Also, after previewing a home, create a name for it, such as "the yellow walls house."

(4) **Open House Instructions.** If you see an Open House Sign, you can view the property without us. As soon as you walk through the door, show our business card and sign in using our name and phone number. If you like the home, do not let the Realtor® know. Call us immediately.

(5) **Signs On Lawns.** If you see a sign on a lawn, and the home was not on the list we sent you, it is either sold or does not have your minimum search requirements. Real estate companies keep the sign up until Settlement. Email us the property address and phone number on the sign. We will find the information for you.

(6) **For Sale By Owners.** Never call on a house listed For Sale By Owner. Email the address and phone number and we will call the Seller. First contact must come from us in order for the Seller to pay our fee.

(7) **Update your Ultimate Scenario.** Communicate with us in detail what you like and dislike about each home you look at, i.e., the floor plan, size of rooms and how you felt in the home. For example, the flow of the home felt great, but the rooms are small for the furniture we have. After each showing, we will ask you, "Do you want to buy this home?" If not, what didn't you like about the home? If you are not finding homes in your current search that fit your needs, we will continue to tweak your search until we find the perfect match. Also, only have one home in your hand at all times that you are considering.

(8) **Your New Job, House Hunting.** Finding a home effectively is like having another job. You have to make a commitment to the process.

John and Susie were very coachable and followed all of our suggestions. They sold their home in four days netting $28,000. Since their home was pre-inspected, the buyer did not do another inspection. They had two offers on their home. We choose the buyer with the better financials and no seller's assist. This allowed them to submit an offer right away on a very special home they had their eye on. The Seller took their offer and we negotiated a 60-day settlement. John and Susie had plenty of time to save more money and prepare themselves for the big move!

As you can see, it is very important to prepare yourself at least six months before you buy and sell real estate. For more information on how you can have a profitable and stress-free home buying and home selling experience go to:
www.6MonthsBeforeYouBuy.com
and: www.6MonthsBeforeYouSell.com.

About Diane

Diane Cardano-Casacio is an innovative marketing expert with an MBA in Marketing, and she is in the business of marketing residential real estate. As seen on FOX, NBC, ABC and CBS on the Masters of Real Estate show, Diane shows off her creative ideas with her *"Coming Soon! 6 Months Before You Sell"* marketing system. Diane explains how her proven marketing systems guarantee her clients bankable results and an opportunity to net more than 18% more in a real estate transaction.

Diane's career in the Real Estate business started when she was just five years old. Diane spent many Sundays at the sample home with her father, Jim Cardano, a licensed Broker and Custom Home Builder. She helped her father by giving prospective buyers a tour of the sample home with innocent passion. A born salesperson, Diane was her dad's top sales agent at age five.

As a child, one of Diane's most admirable qualities was her competitive mind-set. Her desire to excel in everything she did carried her through basketball championships, golf tournaments, a 4.0 student in high school and college, and then after college into Corporate America.

After eight years of feeling trapped by her "Corporate America Job," in 1993 Diane became a licensed Realtor and took control of her own destiny. However, she never outgrew her competitive mindset which translated to her becoming Rookie of the Year –selling 18 homes in her first 6 months as a Realtor – when an experienced agent only sells an average of 4 homes in a full year.

Diane's competitive drive pushed her to start her own boutique real estate company, Cardano Real Estate Experts. Now, her small Team of Expert Consultants sell hundreds of homes a year, year after year, with their main focus being to protect their client's real estate asset.

Diane's unique "6 Months Before You Sell" marketing system is called *"Coming Soon Listings"* and when implemented, guarantees to sell a home for up to 18% more. Diane holds monthly Home Seller Seminars, teaching the eight strategies home sellers must follow to sell their home four times faster than the average and have a stress-free process. Diane's main focus is to maximize her client's net profit by effectively fighting the Home Selling

Sharks. The hundreds of success stories are proof that home sellers must be prepared when selling their home by educating themselves about the home-selling process.

It is results like these that should compel you to pick up the phone and "Call Diane Now" when you get the first thought of selling your home, and see if your home qualifies for her Coming Soon Listing system. Call Diane or go to: www.6MonthsBeforeYouSell.com for your Free Kit explaining the eight Strategies you must have in place six months before you list your home on the market.

If you are not a PA resident, call Diane and she will introduce you to an Expert Consultant in your area. Not happy with the Cardano Experts Team, don't worry, you can fire us at any time after 30 days on the market.

Also, Diane and her Team hold Buyer workshops where first time buyers can learn how to create a profitable, stress-free home buying process and are educated about the different loan programs available. Diane guarantees that if her client is not happy with the home they purchased, she will sell it for free if it's within the first year of ownership. With guarantees like that, when selling or buying real estate, you need to go to: www.CallDianeNow.com to maximize your profits!! Isn't that what it is all about!!

Check out Diane's video blog: www.DianesVideoBlog.com for tons of testimonials, stories, marketing ideas and much more!

CHAPTER 10

Internet Dating For Your House

By Jim Dutton

Getting your house ready for selling - and ready for its MLS debut - is a bit like getting ready for Internet dating after being married for 20 years. Think of this as Match.com for your house! Prospective buyers are your potential suitors; they must be enticed to approach you for the first date, so your profile needs to reflect your home's best attributes.

A friend of mine recently began dating again after the disintegration of her marriage. Within days of her announcing her new "back-on-the-market" status came the consultations with friends, both male and female, as to what personal hygiene and wardrobe issues needed correction first. What emerged was a to-do list of long-overdue maintenance and improvements that had either been over-looked or ignored in the previous 10 years of married life. Some suggestions such as "have you considered finding another colorist for your hair?" came from friends who had taken notice but who didn't want to say anything while my friend was still attached to her spouse. Other vital pieces of advice came from professionals like her therapist, who admonished her to "let go of the sentimental items that represented her past." A relative or two asked her if she was planning to change her wardrobe at all, and mentioned that she had been dressing a little "frumpy" of late.

Any of this dating advice will serve you well in preparing your home for its internet-dating debut. Your job as the seller is to lose your attachment to your house as your home, and begin seeing it as someone else's potential residence. After you begin detaching yourself from your house, your job is to coach your home onto the market. Think about the first thing you take into account when you see someone in person or on a dating site - you consider his or her appearance. What will a potential buyer see first when they search the multi-listing service (MLS) for a home? Buyers tend to rule out first by price.

PRICE

Pricing your home correctly for your market is paramount. In order to sell quickly, you need to be the bullseye. Begin by looking at the absorption rate – how many houses like yours are on the market versus how many have sold each month. This predicts how well your house will sell at a particular value. If you need to sell in X days, you must be realistic about expectations. Conversely, if you have found your new dream house and want to move from your current residence, you may have a little more leeway with pricing. You should be able to tell within the first 2-3 weeks if you have priced your home correctly – based on the number of showings your home receives.

What else affects the price of your home? Certain amenities do make a difference; a new kitchen or bathroom with upgrades will net you more in the sale. Yet, while amenities are important, they are not the first things your potential buyer will see. Amenities usually will not bring them to the door. Your home needs to present well to entice buyers to peek inside and get to know your home.

As mentioned previously, when a person begins dating again after a relationship, the first thing most will do is to spruce up their looks. Few people want to date the person who desperately needs a haircut because you cannot see their eyes, or who is wearing severely-outdated clothing. If you wouldn't look that way to date, you also wouldn't list your house in that condition. What you need is curb appeal!

OUTSIDE: CURB APPEAL

Look at the front of your home from the street. Take a picture (they do not lie), and really see what a potential buyer will see. Does your home's "hair" in the form of trees or shrubs obscure the front of the dwelling? Is the lawn freshly manicured? Are there patches where the turf is missing? You would probably trim your hair, get a manicure or cover the gray if you were going to begin dating again. Step #1 is to clean up your yard and give everything a good trim. Step #2 examines the exterior paint color. Depending on your area, very dramatic colors are probably an unwise choice for your home's exterior. Step three: plant some colorful flowers and plants. Getting ready to date often involves a new wardrobe to spruce up one's image. Your house deserves no less. No one will want to date your house if it is wearing 1970's colors and has hair in its eyes.

After adjusting your home's color and sprucing up the yard, there are a few other inexpensive things you can do to increase curb appeal: pressure wash driveways and sidewalks, repair any exterior trims and windowsills, make sure mailbox is in good repair, and wash all windows that will look better from the street as well as offer more light inside. Additionally, you might consider consulting with a professional who can offer suggestions as to what improvements will make the largest impact. Think of these final additions as the jewelry for your house; you want just enough to make a statement without being gaudy.

INSIDE: BUYER'S PERSPECTIVE

When you are certain that your house has curb appeal, it is time to venture inside to see what a buyer will see. You must have several fresh sets of eyes offer you their objective opinions about your house at this time. Over time and with daily exposure we cease to see the emerging imperfections of our own home, in the same way that one might not notice the gradual graying of a loved one.

De-Clutter: Remove items from all smooth surfaces. Remove all personal photos and items that make your home too personal. Would you date someone who was recently divorced who still had photos of his or her ex-spouse all over the house? It might be hard for you to envision yourself in that person's life as the third wheel. The same will happen with your house if it reflects too much of you. A buyer might not be able to see himself and his life in your home.

Stage: Add or remove furniture from rooms as needed. You never want so much furniture in the room that it appears small, without open spaces in which to move. Now might be a good time to store the excess with a friend or in a storage unit. Kitchens and bathrooms are focal points during a home showing. If you can update only one room, choose the kitchen or bathroom. Adding granite or another smooth surface countertop will bring your room into the 21st century and buyer-dating ready. Now is the time to put away all the small appliances and that kitchen canister set that Grandma gave you in 1991 and let the great bones of your kitchen shine through.

Lighting: Turn on all the lights! You want your home to appear as light and bright as possible. Open blinds, shutters, and curtains to let natural light in and to allow the potential buyer see the beautiful views from your rooms.

Color: If you can afford to re-paint rooms in your home to give an inexpensive facelift, select friendly, inviting colors. Think 'spa colors' such as soft pastel and whites. Add rolled towels and candles in the bathroom, so that the room subtly draws your buyers in and invites them to relax and stay awhile.

With your home now light, friendly, and inviting, it is time to capture its look for the world to see. You will now need to upload photos for the MLS listing and now is not the time for grainy, scanned Poloroid photos.

PHOTOS

Once you have maximized your home's profile for its Internet debut, you will want superior photos and/or video to give propects an accurate depiction of your home's interior and exterior. Listing that your home has architectural windows equates to telling someone that you have blue eyes. Blue eyes are just blue eyes until you see a picture of Liz Taylor's blue eyes! Wouldn't you rather see those blue eyes in person? Show them a spectacular picture of the floor to ceiling architectural windows with the view of the valley below and you just captured your audience. Remember the laws of attraction in dating. You want people to want to date your house; therefore, you do not want to snap the photos of your new, bright, and airy kitchen during a thunderstorm. Close is not good enough here. Excellent, clear, digital photos are a minimal goal. If you can enhance the buyer's experience by offering a 360-degree video peek at the interior of your house or video that highlights the tranquil sound of the waterfall into your pool, you are bound to increase the number of showings.

SHOWINGS

When your home is on the market, you must have it ready to show at a moment's notice. If you have children and plenty of toys lying around, get a decorative chest into which you can toss them for a showing. Add fresh flowers with pleasant, but not overwhelming, scents to add to a vase or two. If you have pets, remove them and the pet fare they leave behind before your home showing. Cats likely can hide themselves, but if you have a dog, take it with you when you leave the house. When your Realtor calls to say that your home will be seen later today, leave the house well before the buyers arrive. You want them to be able to speak freely while they attempt to see themselves making your house their home. If you have small children who will make it hard to go too far, enlist the help of a neighbor, and go stay with them for a short time. Perhaps you and the kids can come and visit for a half hour or so while the Realtor shows your property.

BENEFITS OF HIRING PROFESSIONALS

While you can certainly achieve many of the above goals yourself, there are benefits to hiring professionals to guide you. Professional stagers have a trained eye to see your home the way a buyer would. They can assess your home, your rooms for the correct flow of furnishings and décor to direct the buyers' eyes toward certain features, and away from others. A professional photographer can correct lighting and has the proper tools to enhance your home for its internet dating profile on the MLS. Moreover, a Realtor is more than just someone who can bring buyers to your home. A Realtor will help you realize your goal of selling your home in the timeframe that works best for you and your family.

While working with any of these professionals, bear in mind that your taste may differ from what is currently the trend. Try not to take suggestions personally when your professional recommends a change of color or furniture or price. If you can, recall what you saw the last time you toured a model home. Professionals probably created that look that you fell in love with in the model home – they can do this for your home as well.

Professionals can save you both time and money. Selecting a palate of colors with which to re-paint your home can be daunting, and a pro will know which colors will add emphasis in the right ways. Consider the time invested in photographing your home over the course of a weekend, only to realize when you upload those photos that the lighting is all wrong and that your sage green walls look olive green. Now you have to take all those pictures again! Finally, while you can sell your home "By Owner" the benefits to hiring a professional Realtor to do it for you might outweigh the commission you will pay. Fees for getting your home on the MLS, costs of signage, flyers or newspaper/internet advertising and the chance that you might price yourself out of the right market become exponential when your house does not sell in the timeframe you need.

Preparing your house to return to the market to woo a new family to love it and make it their home requires more than just a quick once-over with a vacuum and dust mop. You may look at your home and think its cracked exterior gives "character" or that the red dining room is "vibrant." A buyer might see the cracks as "delapidated" and the red paint as "loud." Assemble a team of professionals, or at the very least competent friends, who pledge to look at your home objectively, in the same manner a prosective buyer would.

Your team will assess paint colors, curb appeal, and staging of your home. They can then photograph your home to present it in an appealing fashion for your home's upcoming internet-dating debut on the MLS. A buyer's initial search for a home will be much like an initial search on a dating site: what age range are your seeking (or how expensive in the case of the home), what is the zip code, and male or female (in the case of the house, maybe single story or two-story). If the price is right, the buyer might continue and look at the profile. Priced correctly, you stand a better chance of staying in the game long enough to get a date, or showing. Then, with the right attributes, your home's personality will sell itself.

About Jim

Jim Dutton's abundant experience as a Real Estate broker at JD Realty in Los Angeles, CA enables him to expertly guide his clients through a plethora of real estate scenarios. Jim is a member of the National Association of Realtors, The California Association of Realtors, and the National Association of Expert Advisors.

In his 22 years in the industry, Jim lived the dramatic changes in Real Estate as Realtor®, property manager and investor. His passion for Real Estate merged with his B.S. in Marketing and Management from Defiance University propelled Jim and JD Realty to prominence in the Industry.

His designations include: CHSA — Certified Home-Selling Advisor, CDPE — Certified Distressed Property Expert and CNE — Certified Negotiation Expert

Jim's belief in the American Dream of home ownership drove him to create a success plan for a home seller that is both concise and easy to follow.

CHAPTER 11

Contracts And Negotiations

By Bob Eberle

It is becoming very difficult to buy or sell a house in this current economy. Buyers are not able to obtain a loan as easily as they could a few years ago. At a minimum, they need to have good credit, steady work history, verifiable income, and enough assets to cover a down payment and closing costs. As a buyer's agent, it is our job to reduce the cost to the buyer and get them the best deal possible.

It is imperative that you have an agent that has learned the art of negotiation. It is important that you have someone on your side that will learn your wants and needs, and will know how to get it. One can learn a lot about negotiations from a toddler. A four-year old knows what they want, and will not take no for an answer. You need someone with that same mindset and drive in your corner.

I first learned the art of negotiating while setting up multi-million dollar deals for a national oil company as a Territory Sales Manager. My job was to fill the gas stations with people to lease them. Before I could start negotiating, I had to do my homework and learn the parameters from my company. I needed to find out what the minimum the company would take in rent and gas volume. In Real Estate, this first step would be: what is the most you would pay for this house if you are representing the buyer, and what is the lowest you will sell your house for if you represent the seller.

Once I found prospective clients who would be good candidates I would take them out to lunch. It was there that I learned not to negotiate, but to have conversations with prospective clients. We were in a casual, friendly environment, and I would start probing, writing down their response on a napkin. I would ask what they were trying to accomplish. They might have additional usage for the building (car wash, quick lube, etc.). If they did, then they would most likely make more money, and I would know I could get a higher rent. I would also ask what they were looking for (new pumps, signs, free use of credit card); this gave me leverage to start a give-and-take.

Once I understood the other side, I would write down a proposal on the back of a second napkin (giving them upgraded pumps, sign, free use of company credit card in return for a significantly higher rate than the company's minimum gallon requirement). Once the proposal was written I would ask them to come to my office to make it official, and the deal was history. It was really quite simple, know going in what the parameters were, find out what the other side was trying to accomplish without making promises, and draw up a proposal that was a win-win for both sides.

TYPES OF NEGOTIATIONS

Realtors are required to use a contract approved by the board and the state. Many people are not very creative; they simply just fill in the blanks, but you are not limited to that. There are two types of negotiations that I like to use; the first is called the 'Take-away' negotiation, the second is a Dual offer.

1. Take-away Negotiation

With this type of negotiation, buyers start off asking for as much as possible. This way they have more room to negotiate. If you give some items back to the seller, you can get something in return.

For example, a typical asking for more or take-away negotiation would look like this:

When we go into the house we make an inventory of items that could possibly be in play. Typically all the appliances will be included except for the washer and dryer. Look in the garage. Is there a lawn mower, snow blower, etc.? Is there a play set, shed or basketball hoop in the yard? Include everything in the contract that a buyer may want and or need, even if on the listing it says it is excluded. Ask for more than is needed or wanted.

Next, come up with a number that you are willing to pay and would offer on the house. Find out the high/low. A poor agent is going to try and get you to write the high number so that the transaction comes to a conclusion quickly and they get paid. A good agent does not need this transaction to close quickly because they have a steady stream of business. They will take the time to work with you to get you the best deal possible.

Figure out what items in the contract are usual and customary for the buyer to pay, because we are going to ask for the seller to pay those. Our goal is to weight the contract in our favor as much as possible. They key to negotiations is to ask. You don't ask, you don't get.

When the seller's see this offer they will immediately say "NO, this does not work for me", and that will open up the negotiation. They will take away some of the terms you asked for, and want to raise the price. When they do that you will have the power to say I can raise the price but I want to keep some of the terms. In the end you have received added value, getting much more than you would have under ordinary circumstances.

2. Dual Offer Negotiation

With a dual offer, you give the seller two options, A or B, so it moves from a yes/no situation to an A/B situation. Both offers would pose different strengths for both the buyer and seller.

Offer A would be more of a typical offer:

Buyer offers $180,000 on a house listed for $200,000. They get their own mortgage from a bank. Seller would get cashed out at closing and the buyer would get a better price on the house.

Offer B is an owner financed offer:

Buyer agrees to pay full offering price of $200,000 and would assume seller's mortgage payment on a $150,000 existing mortgage. The buyer gives a second mortgage to the homeowner to cover the $50,000 difference at closing. This would lower closing cost for buyer, allow them to close quickly with no money down and they would not have to apply for a mortgage at a bank. Seller would gets his home sold for full asking price and has created a debt instrument which will bring in monthly cash over a long period of time.

About Bob

Bob Eberle has been in the real estate industry for over 26 years. He worked with over 1,200 transactions, with more than 500 of them as a principal. These transactions included foreclosure purchases, owner financing, lease options, situations of collateral and much more.

Bob's real estate career started out in the commercial field. He has more than 9 years experience in the retail marketing/real estate division at Getty Petroleum Corp.

Then he started a career as a real estate investor. Bob flipped houses for 13+ years. In 2006 he was a finalist to star on "Flip This House," A & E's hit television show. Bob then became the President and co-Founder of the New York State Real Estate Investors Association.

He is currently a licensed principal broker of The Real Estate Experts located in upstate New York. Prior to starting his own real estate firm, Bob was a mega agent at Keller Williams, running the Eberle Team for over four years.

Bob has long been known as an expert in the field of real estate. He has been interviewed and featured in many local and national magazine and newspaper articles, been a guest on several radio shows and Internet programs. He has also been featured on television including segments as a guest expert on the topic of real estate for YNN News Channel 9 Time Warner TV, and WTEN News Channel 10.

For more information on Bob Eberle, or if you're interested in buying or selling real estate in the Capital Region, New York, visit: www.AlbanyHomes411.com or call his office at 518-786-7007.

CHAPTER 12

Common Mistakes Smart Buyers Make and How to Avoid Them

By David Kent

Buying a house is a big financial commitment, and for most people, the largest investment they will make in their lifetime. It seems like common sense, but many people jump into the process without really educating themselves first. In the excitement of house hunting they skip over the homework and planning, leaving them vulnerable in the long run. Reading this book is an excellent step in making sure you are prepared.

I have a unique perspective as I have worked exclusively with buyers since 1995. I opened Charleston's first exclusive buyer's agent with my business partner after a career in building. Since opening the Real Buyer's Agent (www.Charlestonhome.com), I have worked with hundreds of buyers and have come across just about every problem you can imagine, and some you probably cannot. Here is a list of the five most common mistakes I see from homebuyers.

COMMON MISTAKE #1:

Not understanding agency. What does agency mean to you? Buyers often do not understand how they can be represented when they buy a house. They make the common mistake of thinking one agent works the same as the next and they do not understand the legality of agency or how agency affects them. Buyers drive around, see a house they think looks interesting and call the number on the 'For Sale' sign. This means they are calling the listing agent who is representing and works for the seller. Do not be one of those people!

The seller's agent owes you no loyalty or confidentiality, and in fact is obligated under law to tell the seller pertinent information you disclose. If you do decide to use the same agent as the seller, you will not have someone to be your advocate. Many states allow designated, dual and transactional agency, which will affect the advice and counsel the agent can give you. This is not the ideal way to ensure that your interests are being protected. Think about it this way, if you are involved in a lawsuit, would you want to use the same attorney as the other side? Do you think that one person can really represent both sides equally? Many homebuyers do not understand that they have a choice and it is up to them to make sure they are represented the way that is best for them.

Prudent buyers plan ahead and go to a real estate company to seek out an agent before starting the process. Because you are reading this book, you will know that single agency is the best choice. Under single agency, an agent only represents one side of the transaction and owes their client fiduciary duties, such as obedience, loyalty, disclosure, confidentiality, accountability, reasonable care, and diligence. Choosing an agent that will act as a buyer's agent and represent only you throughout the transaction is really the best practice.

Organizations like the National Buyer's Agent Alliance (www. buyersagent.net) can put you in touch with a buyer's agent if you're not familiar with the area in which you are considering buying. The organization's primary purpose is to spread the word on buyer's agency and put potential buyers in touch with buyer's agents. Buyers deserve the same representation that the seller receives from their agent. As a buyer, you deserve to have someone fighting on your behalf and acting as your advocate throughout the process and it is up to you to make sure you have it!

COMMON MISTAKE #2:

In addition to understanding types of representation, buyers need to make sure to select the right real estate agent. Mistake number two is not doing your homework up front and picking an agent who is best for you. When you find an agent who you think might be a good fit, interview him or her. How long have they been in the business? Are they a full time real estate agent? Do they have any designations or experience that makes them better suited for your needs? Can they represent you as an exclusive buyer's agent? How much of their business is devoted to listings and how much to representing buyers?

Ideally, you should work with an exclusive buyer's agency where everyone works only with buyers. If that option is not available where you plan to buy, make sure that the agent is willing to represent only you throughout the transaction. Ask for referrals from their past clients and how they will be compensated. Most buyer's agents are paid through a commission split with the listing agent; however, you should discuss other ways that he or she can be compensated. Typically, having your own agent won't cost you more. A good agent will not only represent you, but will educate you throughout the process. It is also the agent's job to use his or her expertise to think of factors and considerations you may not know or have forgotten about.

COMMON MISTAKE #3:

The third common mistake is failing to get pre-approved before looking at homes. For the majority of buyers today, getting a mortgage is an important part of the home-buying process. Getting pre-approved is especially important for first time homebuyers, but it is something that anyone embarking on a house hunt should do. (If you haven't worked with a loan officer/mortgage professional before, your buyer's agent can give you referrals.)

Pre-approval involves contacting a mortgage professional and giving them both some financial and personal information. You will also discuss what kind of monthly payment you would like and the amount of your down payment on your future home. Your mortgage professional will then get you "pre-approved" with a lender for the maximum amount you will be eligible for from that particular lender.

Getting pre-approved enables you to know the price range of homes you will be able to purchase and eliminates the homes that do not fit within your budget. When you find a house that you are ready to put an offer on, a pre-approval letter can show the seller that you are serious and have the ability to obtain financing required to purchase the house they are selling. In a nutshell, it will save you time looking only at homes you are comfortable financing and will put you in a better negotiating position.

Keep in mind that the lender who provides your pre-approval letter does not need be the same lender who finances your mortgage. You still have the ability to shop for the best rate and terms when the time comes.

COMMON MISTAKE #4:

Number four on the common mistakes list is concentrating first on individual properties rather than the location of the property. Many buyers get caught up in looking at particular homes on the Internet or having their agent take them to numerous homes without much focus or thought. If you find your dream house, but it does not fit your work, shopping or school needs, then you are not going to be happy there! Until you narrow down the area that fits you and your family best, you are wasting your time looking at homes.

If you are not familiar with the areas, it is perfectly OK to go look at a few homes in several areas, with the goal of these excursions being location focused. Here are some important things to consider when thinking about the area:

- What are your priorities?
- Where do you spend the majority of your time?
- How far is the property to your job and what is the potential commute time?
- How does the school's performance compare to similar schools in the area?

Even if you do not have school-age children, school performance can play a significant role in home re-sales. If you do have children, take the time to look up the schools-testing results and graduation percentages and plan school visits. When you go to sell this home, school performance is a factor that future buyers may consider and can play a part in how long it takes for a house to sell.

In addition to the factors that have to do with your lifestyle, also consider environmental factors that are going to affect the price of the property. Every area is different. However, in the Charleston area where I work, the distance the property is to a beach or the downtown area greatly affects price, not only in the initial cost of the property, but also in additional expenses like flood insurance and wind and hail insurance. The closer you are to the water, the more expensive it is.

Check with your agent to see what environmental factors might come into play in the areas you are considering. You should also consider the Census data. Is the area you are considering purchasing economically healthy? What does job growth look like? What industries are strong? What kind of crime does a particular area have? Contacting the local police station and asking for a crime report is a great way to really know what's going on in a particular area.

Check to see how many foreclosures/short sales there are in the neighborhood you're considering. At the end of the day, you need to make sure that you have done everything in your control to ensure that you are picking an area that will nurture appreciation for your future home and is a place you will be happy and enjoy for years to come. Once you have tackled this, then concentrate on the homes that meet your requirements from the research you have done.

COMMON MISTAKE #5:

Ok, so you have picked an agent and know you have got the best representation possible. You have done your research on the area, found a house, negotiated the terms. Common mistake number five is not getting a home inspection. It is amazing to me how many people want to skip this important step. Buying property is a big commitment, and until an appraisal and inspection have been done, you really do not know for sure what you are getting. Not all defects are visible to the untrained eye, and frankly, the majority of people don't know everything to be considered.

Keep in mind all home inspectors are not created equal. Much like picking an agent to represent you, make sure you are picking a qualified inspector. I highly recommend you use someone who is insured and certified by an organization such as with the American Society of Home Inspectors (www.ashi.org). You want an inspector who has been trained and has the necessary knowledge and expertise to give you a through inspection. You are not looking for some guy who was just laid off, owns a pickup and suddenly decides, "Maybe I'll start doing inspections; how tough can it be?" Using an inspector who is certified gives you more recourse if you have a problem in the future.

Buying new construction does not exempt you from needing a top-flight home inspection. A home inspection is cheap insurance that can save you significant money and problems that were built into the house. I recommend, at a minimum, both a pre-drywall and a final inspection for new construction. During the pre-drywall inspection, the electrical, plumbing, and ductwork can be inspected prior to the instillation of the sheet rock, which is a real benefit over resale properties as the walls are already in place. The final inspection covers the five major components of a home: structural integrity, roof, electrical, plumbing and heating and air-conditioning.

With a thorough inspection, you will know the real cost of the property and what kind of projects you would be taking on if the seller refuses to do repairs. Having an inspection enables you to negotiate some repairs or, at the very least know what things could be eating away at the equity of a property. If you can get the seller to take care of the major items from the repair list, you will be in that much better of a position when it comes time for you to sell the house. In addition to the home inspection, depending on the area where you are buying, you may also want to consider radon, lead paint, septic, mold, water sampling, etc. Your agent can help recommend which of these might be pertinent depending on the house location and age.

Avoiding these common mistakes and making sure you have got a team of trustworthy people working for you will help you to make a great buy. The home buying process is full of unexpected surprises but working with a buyer's agent can make the process a lot less stressful and a lot more enjoyable for you. I've had clients say that using a buyer's agent to help buy their home "exceeded every expectation" they had about buying property. You deserve this experience when you buy your home.

So to recap, here are the most common mistakes every homeowner should avoid:

1. Not Understanding Agency
 • Choosing a buyer's agent who will represent your interests throughout the transaction is the best choice.

2. Choosing the Wrong Real Estate Agent: Do you your Homework!
 • Interview potential agents. Ask questions. Check past performance.

3. Not Getting Pre-approved
 • You'll know what payment you're comfortable with and you'll be in a better negotiation position when you find the right house.

4. Location, Location, Location: Pick the location before the house
  - You'll save yourself time and end up with a property you'll be happy with in the long run.

5. Not having a Home Inspection
  - Know the true cost of the property and what you're really taking on. In addition you'll be in a better position when you sell the house.

About David

A graduate of Clemson University, with a B.S. in Building Science and Construction Management, David Kent has worked on many subdivison developments and building projects. In 1995, with his distinctive background and extensive knowledge of the real estate industry, David Kent decided to embark on a new path. David and his business partner W.C. "Cece" Stricklin, opened Charleston's first exclusive buyer's agency, The Real Buyer's Agent (www.charlestonhome.com). Steadfast and committed to buyer representation, this relatively new approach to the real estate business took flight. For over a decade, David and his team of agents consistently provided clients with fervent representation and superior service.

David is also committed to further education about buyer representation and elevating the standards within the real estate profession. In 1998, he received his Accredited Buyer Representative (ABR) status and in 2000, his Accredited Buyer Representation Managers (ABRM) status. He has acted on the Real Estate Buyer's Agent Council (REBAC) advisory board since 2008, and helped to re-write the ABR course in 2009. He has acted as the President of the Charleston Trident Association of Realtors, the President of the Multiple Listing Service for the Charleston Trident Association of Realtors, as well as the Charleston Trident Homebuilders Association.

In 2008, he was voted Realtor Of The Year by the Charleston Trident Association of Realtors. He has also acted as a Director for the National Association of Realtors and was named to the 2009 National Association of REALTORS Leadership Academy. In 2010, he was inducted to the (REBAC) Real Estate Buyer's Agent Council Hall of Fame. Currently, David is the acting South Carolina Realtors Education Foundation (REF) President.

CHAPTER 13

One Stop Shop…The Easy Approach to the Home Buying Process

By Jeff Cook

Meet Ben and Emily. They are newlyweds and are looking to buy a home. They have always been told by family and friends that owning a home is better than renting, but they are overwhelmed at the idea and don't know where to begin. Family members have told them about equity appreciation, the tax benefits and the freedom of owning their own place that they can call home. Seems easy, right? But, Ben and Emily are just like most other buyers and are more intimidated about the paperwork and the process to buy the home than they are about actually moving into and living in the home.

The pain is in the process of purchasing, not the actual purchase itself, particularly for first time buyers or buyers who haven't experienced the process in sometime, and are getting back into the game.

- What should Ben and Emily expect in terms of fees and down payments?

- How do they find their perfect home, negotiate the best deal, and what do all the papers mean that they are expected to sign?

• Wouldn't it be better if there was a solution from a realtor to solve all of these problems in one place (a One Stop Shop) vs. them having to frantically stress amongst all the details and all the people that may be involved?

Well, I helped Ben and Emily buy their first home when they got married and that was actually four years ago. It turned out pretty well for them because sometime ago, they came back to me to help them buy a bigger home, and have since started a family and have a newborn boy in that new home!

As for Ben and Emily, the most difficult steps of the home buying process are:

(a). Finding the right property

(b). Coordinating paperwork

(c). Understanding the process and steps of the transaction

(d). Assisting with negotiations

In fact when polled, 55% of home buyers responded that the most important aspect that they look to a realtor to assist them in is finding the right home and 25% responded to help with price negotiations and other negotiations of the terms of the sale.*

So what is the solution for today's homebuyer that is simply looking for an easy strategy to maximize the home-buying process, but is looking to avoid the hassle and painstaking process? We've created the The Ultimate Homebuyer Strategy that takes a Real Estate team approach, and allows the consumer to benefit from the different minds, resources, and talents of that team under a One-Stop Shop environment. This means that the homebuyer can get Realty services, negotiations, home searches, mortgages, credit repair, contract explanation, title insurance, homeowners insurance, and attorney services all under one roof at Jeff Cook Real

*(National Assoc. of Realtors Profile of homebuyers and sellers)

Estate. So long to the confusing days of hiring multiple different professionals to help serve you in the home-buying process. We have created a brief but detailed action plan below to help you confidently approach the rigors of the home-buying process.

Our sole objective is to make your home-buying experience the absolute best it can be. We do this by helping you find the best home, helping you negotiate the best price, helping you secure the best financing and monthly payments, protecting you throughout the entire process, and making the entire process as hassle free as possible. Our program is a one-stop shop and is entirely free to you! The seller pays all of our fees. If for any reason you are not happy within the first year, we will re-sell that home for free on our part.

Who should you have to represent you during the home purchase? If you call the real estate agent that has the home listed to represent you, you are paying that agent to negotiate against you. They represent the seller! Using an exclusive buyer's agent, you know you have an agent that will represent you and your best interest at all times.

Our smart homebuyer system was designed with you in mind and is different to anything else you have seen. We focus exclusively on your needs during the process. It is comprised of five simple steps: Home Loan Pre-Approval, Finding the Right Home for You, Negotiating the Best Price and Terms, Protecting Your Interests, and you get a Real Estate Advisor for Life!

If needed, we have dedicated lender experts on our team to advise you of the best financing for you. Not all loans are right for everyone. We find the perfect match for you. We want you to know how much home you can comfortably afford and put you in the strongest purchasing position to know how much to offer on a home within your specific limits.

Are you ready to go shopping for your perfect home? The MLS has thousands of homes for sale from all participating Real

Estate companies. Therefore, we have access to all homes for sale from each different real estate office in town, all foreclosure homes, and new construction build-out homes. Many other agents still operate on the "old school" mentality: by making a random search, picking out six or ten houses for you to see, and then pressure you to buy one of them. The problem with this approach is that the wrong person is picking out your home, and most buyers are savvy enough to not settle for this type of high-pressure sales technique! Our solution is designed for you to view only homes that are pertinent to you and your needs!

We alert you of hottest new listings that match your criteria, give you priority access to new listings and make your search simple and quick. We do this with our customized smart search by entering in specific information that you want in a home and you are automatically notified instantly when a new listing comes out that may interest you. No more viewing homes that don't have what you are shopping for! We only send you homes that match your specific criteria, you pick out as many as you like and drive by them, when you see one you like, call us and we'll arrange a private showing. There is NO pressure to buy and the search can be modified at any time! No more overpaying for a home you like because you can beat out other buyer's. You are notified instantly and often before anyone else even knows it's on the market. We don't waste time viewing homes that are already sold or that another agent has picked out for you. This home finder system is custom-built specifically for you and often you can save thousands with foreclosure options or other distressed or new construction build-out homes!

When you find the home you want, we will help you negotiate the best price and terms, help prepare that offer and present it to the seller on your behalf, and help negotiate the terms acceptable to you. Say goodbye to the days of high-pressure sales similar to the used car industry. We make this simple by consulting with you then we go to work on the other side to negotiate for your best interest. There are various closing costs and attorney fees that we can help get the seller to pay on your behalf. Most home buyers think it is as simple as finding a home and coming up with a price to offer but indeed the sales contract (offer to purchase) is 7-8 pages long with details about inspection costs, move-in dates, closing fees, realtor representation etc. Our job is to help you facilitate this experience and since we deal with this same purchase contract on a daily basis, we know all of the ins and outs for your advantage! When we're done negotiating the exact terms, you'll be in escrow on your new home with terms that are 100% acceptable to you!

After you've contracted the home, we want to make sure that you get the home that you expect, so we work to protect your interests during this process. We help make sure the house is in a condition acceptable to you and let you know all information that affects the value and livability of the home by reviewing pertinent seller disclosures, etc. We recommend several competent affiliates (inspectors, etc.), to work with you during your due diligence period to make sure that the home is acceptable. This due diligence period takes place before you are committed to the purchase, because we structure your sales contract in such a way that allows easy exit if we run into turbulence along the way.

Trivia Question: How many people are involved in the average real estate transaction from the beginning of the process until the end? Fifty-two! Think about it… you have agents, inspectors, appraisers, loan officers, bank personnel, attorneys, paralegals, plus everyone on the seller's side of the transaction to deal with all at the same time. For you to try to keep up with all these people would be like trying to herd cats! Our job is to be your liaison during this process, and we have office personnel that coordinate the closing process to make sure all details are completed along the way in preparation for you to take occupancy of your new home!

Usually, agents disappear when the sale is complete. We are real estate advisors for life! After you've moved in, if you decide to paint, or complete upgrades within the home, we have inexpensive service contractors on standby for your reference! As I said in the beginning, we don't charge buyers for these services and we truly have laid out the complete homebuying solution. Our team is on standby ready to assist you with your home purchase here in the Charleston, SC area. Visit: www.JeffCookRealEstate.com for more information.

About Jeff

Jeff Cook is a real estate broker in Charleston-Summerville tri-county area of South Carolina, and is part owner of the second-largest realty company in the Charleston Metro area, The AgentOwned Realty Co.

Jeff was laid off in 2002 in the Corporate America environment for being among the best sales associates, when the company eliminated commission-based sales agents and paid them their average hourly wage.

Jeff rebounded in 2003, graduating both with a bachelor's in business from the University of South Carolina and also from Real Estate University, both within a week of each other. Jeff went on to open his own small business, where he could be rewarded for his honest, hard work and provide a safe goal-oriented work force within his organization. In 2011 and 2012, Jeff was the No. 1 residential resale agent in the Charleston, South Carolina market (non-REO and non-new construction) and is frequently sought out by local media publications, talk shows and local radio stations for his real estate updates.

Jeff is married to the lovely Sarah, and they have a husky-shepherd mix named Johnny.

For more information or to buy a Charleston-Summerville tri-county area home, Jeff can be reached at (843) 608-9520, email:
JeffCook@JeffCookRealEstate.com
Or on the web: www.JeffCookRealEstate.com.

CHAPTER 14

The Pre-Approval Process And Making A Proper Offer

By Lee Tessier

There are literally dozens and dozens of issues that need to be addressed during the house buying process. In this chapter, I would like to focus on the pre-approval process and why this step is foundational to making a proper offer. In fact, this may be one of the most intimidating tasks in the home buying process, but hopefully the information I share with you will help alleviate any anxiety related to this event. As you can imagine, there are numerous questions to be asked, and several documents that will be required to enable you to move through the pre-approval process to open the door to make an offer on a home you desire to purchase. The pre-approval process is extremely important to the buyer, the seller, and the real estate agent. If the buyer is not pre-approved, they may look at dozens of houses and spend countless hours searching for the right home, only to find out they are not qualified to purchase.

The task of purchasing a home doesn't have to be a daunting task if you have the proper direction by enlisting appropriately qualified people to assist you in the process. I cannot stress enough the importance of working with the right people every step of the way to make this experience a pleasant one, and to reduce any potential of something going wrong along the way.

So, before we start discussing the pre-approval process, let me add something about aligning yourself with the right resources that will make the entire process flow as smoothly as possible. Finding the right people is actually a key component to a smooth pre-approval process and making a proper offer.

It is extremely important to understand that not all real estate agents are the same. Yet statistically, 83% of buyers will use the first agent with whom they speak. For example, if you call a Realtor's office and the person taking phone calls that day is the least-experienced agent in the office, you may not be getting the best person to represent you in the transaction. I would recommend that you interview a few real estate agents before making a decision. Ask the potential agent how long they have been in the business, …how many homes they sell a year, …if they are full time or part time, …and how many hours a week they work. The average agent sells between five and seven houses a year, but a highly productive agent will sell much more. In fact, the real estate agents in my office average almost as many sales per month as the average real estate agent completes in one year.

That is the type of real estate agent you should seek out, someone that has a history of a high number of successful transactions. You may also want to search the Internet and find who is doing the most advertising for their business. This alone should not be the reason you enlist them to represent you, but it does tell you if they are serious about their business. You may also want to get a referral from a trusted resource or friend that has used a particular agent in the past. Here is another important question you will want to ask a potential real estate agent who would represent you, "Do you work on a team or do you function in a solo capacity?" An agent plugged into a team of associates that specialize in various components of the buying process will typically be the better choice to represent you. For example, in my office I employ a General Manager, Listing Manager, Transactional Manager, Customer Service Representative, Marketing Specialist, Bookkeeper, five buyer specialists, and one other listing agent (I also function as a listing agent). I created this team because there are so many things that need to be done during the buying process. Each of these individuals plays an extremely important part in getting the buyer from the beginning to the end of the buying process. We make sure things are completed – such as the home inspection, the list of repairs, termite inspection, radon test, specific requirements in the contract, and the list goes on and on.

In contrast, an agent working solo has a greater chance of missing some deadlines because they are trying to handle all the responsibilities of the transaction. If things are not done in a timely manner or if the specific requirements of the contract are not met, the seller could exercise a unilateral release and release the buyer from contract and accept someone else's offer, or it could cause unnecessary delays in the process.

Make sure you also understand the responsibilities of the buyer's agent and what they will be doing for you. The nuances of the buyer's agent may vary from state to state, but the buyer's agent will inform you of their specific responsibilities and how you will benefit from working with them. The buyer's agent should make sure this is done during the first meeting with the buyer.

A good real estate agent will have certain lenders they will recommend based upon your particular circumstances. Their recommendations will depend upon the status of the buyer. For example, an established professional upgrading to a million dollar home from their five-hundred thousand dollar home may receive a different referral than a first time homebuyer who recently graduated from college. A good real estate agent will also know if there are specific grant programs that can assist the buyer if necessary, and direct the buyer to lenders that work with the grant programs. For example, in the city of Baltimore, they have a "Live Near Your Work" program that will assist a homebuyer with a $5,000 to $7,000 grant. I am also aware of one program that offers 2.85% on a thirty-year fixed rate mortgage and they offer additional grant money to assist with house repairs. These types of programs will vary from community to community, and your real estate agent should be aware of what programs are available. Some of these programs require repayment while others are self-forgiving after a certain period of time.

After you have determined the best lender for you, the lender will help you decide the most appropriate loan by asking numerous questions. The most commonly-used loans are conventional, conventional rehab, FHA, FHA 203K, and VA loans. Your lender will be able to help you determine the proper financing for your situation. You will also need to determine how much money you will be able to use as a down payment. The lender will help you determine what size loan and loan payment you will be able to afford – based on your income and your debt to income ratio. That will then determine your house shopping price range.

Regarding down payments, with an FHA loan you will typically need 3.5% of the purchase price as a down payment. If you are looking for a "fix up" type home, your lender may direct you to an FHA 203K loan which allows you to incorporate into the loan a certain amount to be allocated specifically for repairs. In that case, your down payment will be the same 3.5%, but it will be based on the sale price of the home plus the repair cost. Conventional loans today are ranging from 5% to 20% required as a down payment, depending on the lender and the credit score of the borrower. Mortgage insurance is another factor that will influence your payment. If you can put down 20% or more as a down payment on your purchase, you would not have mortgage insurance. However, any down payment less than 20% will require mortgage insurance. Sometimes there will be a pre-paid mortgage insurance option that will make the monthly payment lower, but more often than not, mortgage insurance is paid as part of the monthly mortgage payment. For those that qualify because of their military service, VA loans can be done with 100% financing, including closing costs, and no down payment required. In some instances, the buyer is even able to roll a certain amount of personal debt, such as credit card debt, into the closing costs if the seller is agreeable, and if the house appraises for the necessary amount.

Another factor to consider when determining what loan will be best for you is "Seller Concessions." For example, a seller can give the buyer up to 6% toward their closing costs on an FHA loan. On a conventional loan, the seller can generally give between 3% and 6% toward closing costs – depending on the size of the down payment. Your lender will be able to give you specific information related to seller concessions for specific loan types.

To enable a lender to evaluate the pre-approval of a buyer, the potential buyer will need to provide two years of full tax returns, their last two pay stubs, their last two bank and investment statements, and proof of down payment. The lender, after obtaining your permission, will look at your credit score to determine your credit risk and to determine which lenders will consider you as an acceptable credit risk. The higher your credit score, the more programs for which you will qualify. The converse is also true, the lower your credit score, the fewer programs for which you will qualify. After the loan officer collects all the necessary information about you, they will submit a formal request to one of their underwriters. The underwriter will then make the official determination on behalf of the lender as to the maximum amount they will lend you, your monthly payments, and the length of the loan.

When the pre-approval process is completed, the lender will present the potential buyer with a "Pre-Approval Letter." This letter will indicate to the seller that the buyer has been pre-approved by a lender and that they can afford to purchase the home. It is also important that the buyer ask the lender for both the Good Faith Estimate and the Good Faith Worksheet. The Good Faith Estimate can be somewhat confusing. The Good Faith Worksheet actually helps to clarify the Good Faith Estimate document. These documents will not only outline the specific expenses related to a home purchase, but it will also help the real estate agent determine how to best structure the purchase offer for a home. If an offer is made without consideration of the information contained in these documents, it could be potentially detrimental to the buyer. These two documents are very important to me when I am helping a client write an offer. Unfortunately, not all real estate agents will take the time to understand these documents and the implications they have to the offer, but an experienced agent will fully understand the great value and usefulness of these documents when helping you to make a proper offer.

After the pre-approval process is complete, it is important for your real estate agent to discuss with you specifics regarding the type of home you desire to purchase. Based on the pre-approval letter, what will be the price range of homes for which you will be looking? Regarding location, do you want to be in a specific school district, in a specific neighborhood or subdivision, or within a certain distance from your job? What are the "must haves" as opposed to the "wants" in the home you will be purchasing? How many bedrooms and bathrooms do you require? Do you require granite countertops in the kitchen or is that something you would give up if the house had everything else you required? Other things buyers often list in either a "must have" or "want" category are hardwood floors, fireplace, finished basement, three car garage, and the list will go on depending on your desires. Keep in mind that legally your real estate agent cannot advise a home buyer about a specific neighborhood or school district. However, a buyer can talk with friends and other people within the community to determine if the area is up to the standard they require for living.

After finding the house you want to purchase, your agent will need to contact the listing agent to make sure there isn't a pending contract. It's possible that a listing will show as active on the Multiple Listing Service, but there may already be an offer on the house that is being negotiated. Sometimes the only way to know that is by contacting the listing agent. If there is a pending offer that may mean you will want to submit your best offer as your initial offer. Many states also have laws regarding certain disclosures that must be obtained and revealed to a potential buyer prior to the offer being made. The Listing Agent will be the person responsible for supplying this information.

It is very important to structure your offer so you can maximize the provisions of your pre-approved loan as well as maximize the allowable seller concessions. Your real estate agent will know how to write an offer that will be beneficial to you as a buyer and use every dollar so nothing is lost in the process. This is where an experienced agent will be a huge benefit to you as a buyer. The agent will be able to dissect the Good Faith Estimate and the Good Faith Worksheet you obtained from the lender to make sure you are taking advantage of every dollar available. There are certain situations where if the offer is not structured properly, the seller could end up with additional money that you should have used to your benefit.

If you as the buyer already own a home, you will have to make the offer on the home you want to purchase contingent on the selling of your existing home. The seller then has the option of accepting or rejecting the contingency. If the seller accepts the contingency, then the timing for the contingency needs to be settled. Will the seller agree to a 30 or 45-day contingency to give the buyer time to sell their existing home? Coordinating the details of a contingency offer is often a juggling act because of the restricted timing to sell the buyer's house and then the coordination of the settlement for the house the buyer is selling and the house the buyer is buying. There may also be a need for a seller to request to stay in the house after it has been sold. If that happens, a rent back period and terms will also have to be included in the offer.

The offer will always be structured around the pre-approval document. If the buyer will need assistance with closing costs, that has to be clearly spelled out in the offer and it has to be within the parameters of what is allowable through the type of financing that has been obtained. As alluded to earlier, a seller can give the buyer up to 6% toward their closing costs on an FHA loan, but on a conventional loan, the seller can generally only give between 3% and 6% toward closing costs depending on the size of the down payment. These factors will have to be carefully calculated and included in the offer if deemed necessary by the buyer.

I strongly recommend that a buyer always ask for the seller to pay for a home warranty to protect you against a major expense within the first year of purchasing a home. For example, if the furnace or hot water heater goes out, the home warranty, with a small deductible, will cover the expense of that major repair. Offering a one-year home warranty can also be a selling point that will benefit the seller when they list their house. Buyers often gravitate toward a home that has a home warranty.

Obviously, there are a plethora of details to consider in the real estate buying process. The average non-real estate agent will never remember every detail or be able to keep up with the ever-changing regulation related to the process. But, finding a professional that can guide you through the myriad steps in the buying process can be worth their weight in gold. You will benefit greatly by understanding the basics that I have outlined in this chapter and by connecting with an experienced real estate professional in your area to help guide you through the maze. Remember, the buying process doesn't have to be intimidating if you have the right people on your side.

About Lee

Lee Tessier is a 32-year native of Baltimore and has a great passion for Real Estate. Having worked in the sales industry for more than 23 years, and with 80% of his business from referrals, he is known for following through and getting the job done.

Lee regularly attends conferences and has obtained several professional designations. He is an active member of NAEA (National Association of Expert Advisors). Proving his years of experience, Lee works with investors who handle rehab properties, as well as short sales and foreclosures. Within the past seven years, Lee has successfully served over 650 families, so clients are guaranteed to be working with an experienced Realtor who believes that anytime is the right time to buy or sell.

He and his staff specialize in working with people who are both buying and selling a home, upsizing or downsizing. This takes a little more patience and is much more time consuming than working only one side of a transaction. They have to make sure that both sides are in perfect sync at all times – but this is truly an advantage to you, since they are able to maintain control of most of the variables. They pride themselves on proactive management of the entire process. They understand how to structure a contract for success and then to troubleshoot the details along the way.

His staff is top notch with a combined **60+ years of experience in the industry**. Their experience ensures your most important financial concerns are handled by dedicated professionals, not entry-level staff. Their entire business is based on clearly-defined systems to ensure excellence and consistency in service. Their systems are built so that marketing and communication are both routine and yet innovative. They seek out the newest and most effective means to market your property, with an eye on emerging trends within the industry. This ensures that your property is given the most exposure to the market, with the greatest appreciation for your property's strong points.

CHAPTER 15

Flying High Above Clouded Skies

By Brian Kissinger & Catherine Kaufer

Paulina was referred to HoM SaF System by a local Realtor, Catherine Kaufer, who Brian Kissinger with Hom Saf, has had a great deal of success with – in negotiating Short Sales concessions on behalf of distressed homeowners. Paulina was a different scenario however. She was an investor. In this transaction she was to serve as both a buyer and a seller. By taking an extremely aggressive approach, we utilized all that we had learned in the loss mitigation and foreclosure arena and applied it to the process from the buyer's side. We quickly learned that the same amount of concessions were needed to be made as in a normal Short Sale Transaction, but the concessions were to be made by Paulina, not the lenders. Each and every concession made by Paulina was made for a price. Thousands and thousands of dollars discounted each and every time an issue was identified.

The property Paulina was trying to buy and sell was, unfortunately, a typical one in today's marketplace. Almost $900,000 was owed between the first and second mortgages and the property had a current value between $500,000-$600,000. The first mortgage was with Bank of America, originally Countrywide, and the amount owed was about $700,000. The second mortgage was with Wells Fargo and the amount owed was about $185,000. The current homeowner was laid off from his job, trapped in 2 unaffordable loans that were so typically given during the sub-prime boom. The homeowner was 27 months behind and, although foreclosure had not been filed on him, it was imminent.

Paulina and Catherine already had a well-qualified buyer identified, willing to pay the fair market price of $550,000 for the property.

The results that were obtained by Catherine and HoM SaF System were truly impressive. The total profit was $194,847. The total process was completed in 54 days. The purchase price on the Bank of America mortgage was negotiated down from $700,000 to $310,000. The purchase price on the Wells Fargo mortgage was negotiated down from $185,000 to $30,000. Bank of America agreed to the Wells Fargo payoff. Paulina got around Bank of America's rule prohibiting buyers from "flipping" a property within 90 days. We were able to get Bank of America to waive the remaining balance on the sellers first loan and rights to pursue further deficiency or judgment. We were able to get Bank of America to report the first mortgage as "settled for less than the amount owed" and NOT issue a 1099 to the seller for the difference.

This was all completed in less than 2 months.

Short sales, like virtually everything else in today's dynamic marketplace, are a highly specialized field of endeavor. The speed at which offers are accepted, and most times the very acceptance itself, depends upon how deals are submitted and the ability to understand what the lender is looking for on multiple levels. The first is the actual preparation of documents submitted to the lender. How they are prepared and submitted can shave weeks or even months off the approval process. The best prepared documents are worthless, however if you do not understand what information the lender is looking for on the documents. All short sale offers must fit a certain matrix which varies from lender to lender if they are ever to be accepted. Various state and federal requirements also have to be satisfied. Without this knowledge, investors are doomed to spin their wheels on a transaction that will never actually be finalized. Finally, there is the financial transaction legal discovery that will maximize investor savings on a property. The sellers lender's ability to legally sell the property may be clouded at best and illegal at worst.

Paulina understood the value of working with an aggressive Realtor who was well qualified and experienced in dealing with short sales. Make sure that your agent is well versed or works with an equally aggressive investigation, legal discovery and negotiations firm. Qualifying the team that will enact your transaction should be as important as qualifying the property you wish to purchase itself. Paulina's due diligence in all areas of the process allowed her to relax while her team battled the seller's lender's and she realized a profit of almost $200,000 in under 2 months. Make sure that your agent/negotiator is well versed in the following areas.

I. VARIOUS TYPES OF LOANS & THE PROCESS FOR SHORT SELLING THEM

Fixed Rate, FHA, VA, Option ARM, HELOC, Interest Only and Negative Amortization loans are some of the types of loans that will have to be negotiated in a Short Sale. Within these main categories of loans there are several specialized sub-categories of loans. All of these loan types have different State and Federal requirements which must be satisfied for the process to be finalized. The different loan types all have different payoffs to lenders based on risk at origination. Well-qualified buyers paid a lower return to lenders on a safer loan than did higher risk loans given to less qualified buyers. All of this translates to what an individual investor and a lender were expecting to make on a loan, and what, by extension, they are willing to settle for in compromise. Is the loan Federally insured, securitized, owned by Fanny Mae or Freddy Mac, etc.? This will determine whether this loan qualifies for any Federal or insurance money to offset lender losses in a Short Sale. Knowing whether and how much a lender may be subsidized allows you to have a lower price accepted.

II. WHAT WILL GET APPROVED IN A PURCHASE CONTRACT

Even after a lender approves a short sale, it could require that the seller sign a promissory note to repay the deficient amount of the loan. This probably will not be acceptable to financially desperate sellers. This will cause the seller to back out of the Short Sale which will have wasted your time. Lenders may also try to get the purchaser to accept a property "as is". Having a seasoned Realtor and negotiator is crucial to ensure that none of these potential "deal breakers" are slid into a deal at the last minute. Experience really is the key here as all lenders are different and what may be acceptable to one may not 'fly' with another.

III. LOSS MITIGATION

Unfortunately, most short sale negotiations begin in the Loss Mitigation department of the seller's lender. This means that the lender has, at least preliminarily, made the decision to foreclose on this property, take title back on the property and sell it as REO or in auction. Convincing the lender to accept an offer in compromise and sell it to you can be tricky. Understanding what NET dollar amount needs to be realized by the lender is crucial if the transaction is to be completed by the Loss Mitigation department. Another approach is to identify illegalities associated with the origination and assignment of the loan itself. This will often take the transaction out of the Loss Mitigation department and place it in the legal department of the lender. This is where your Realtor and negotiator are invaluable, as this is where your biggest reductions in price and most favorable concessions will be realized.

IV. WHAT QUALIFIES AS A SHORT SALE PROPERTY

There are a few generally-accepted criteria for what will qualify a property as a viable short sale opportunity. One or more of the following will usually have to exist for the Loss Mitigation departments of lenders to entertain a short sale offer.

1) The homeowner/seller is behind on payments. The property does not have to be in foreclosure, but generally the lender has adopted the 90-day delinquency point as being the starting point for entertaining a short sales offer. This is almost always the point at which the homeowner is in default on his mortgage. This is also the time when most mortgages are assigned to the lenders Loss Mitigation Department.

2) Is the homeowner/seller experiencing financial hardship? Like so many other homeowners, the downturn in the economy has resulted in unemployment which translates to homeowners falling behind on their mortgage payments. Divorce, death of a spouse, the recast of an adjustable rate mortgage are also financial hardships that cause delinquencies. The homeowner/sellers preparation of a hardship letter, as required by the lender, will be crucial in the approval process. If the homeowner does not have assistance in the preparation of this letter, get it for them.

3) Is the property underwater? This simply means does the homeowner/seller owe more on this property than it is currently worth? And is the homeowner insolvent, meaning, unable to make up the difference in a sale between the sale price and the amount owed?

V. NET THRESHOLDS FOR FHA, VA, AND CONVENTIONAL SHORT SALES

Understanding NET Thresholds is the key to the entire short sale process. Based on the insurance on the loan, government or otherwise, the homeowner/sellers lender is guaranteed to recoup a set amount if a foreclosure is completed on a homeowners property. FHA loans are guaranteed 82% of the value of the property. For VA (Veteran Affairs) loans this number is 88% and for conventional loans the lender is guaranteed to recoup 80% of market value on a property if it forecloses. If the Loans are Fannie Mae or Freddie Mac backed, then the guaranteed recoup percentage jumps to 90% and 92% respectively.

VI. DETERMINING MARKET VALUE

Just because the percentages that a lender recoups in a foreclosure are rigid does not mean that the actual dollars are. Determining the B.P.O. (Brokers Price Opinion) on a conventional, Fannie Mae or Freddie Mac loan, the F.M.V. (Fair Market Value) of a VA loan, or the C.A.A. (Certified Appraised Amount) of an FHA loan will make the difference between success and failure for a short sale investor. If your number is higher than the lender will receive in a foreclosure, approval is virtually guaranteed. If not, rework your numbers. It's that simple.

We could write an entire book, and we are, on the variables associated with determining the B.P.O., F.M.V. or C.A.A. of an individual property. What condition is the property in? From what size area are comparables pulled? What repairs are needed on the house? What is the post-repair value? Your Realtor, and by extension, your qualification of that Realtor, is your single best friend for this. The Comparative Market Analysis, home inspections, appraisals and analytics performed by your Realtor can, and did in Paulina's case, earn you hundreds of thousands of dollars.

VII. CLOUDED TITLE AND CONVEYANCE ISSUES

In a rush to securitize loans during the real estate boom from 2000-2008 lenders and servicers were extremely sloppy, and in many cases fraudulent in their selling, assignment and conveyance of mortgages. More and more courts are ruling that, as a result of these inadequate/illegal conveyances, that short sales and foreclosures are illegal because the lender lacked the legal standing to conduct or negotiate the sale. This is resulting in more and more reversals of transactions completed after 2009. Do not let the homeowner/sellers lender pass this problem on to you. A good negotiator/legal discovery company will perform a complete financial transaction risk assessment that will identify any and all financial transaction issues associated with the subject property. No savvy investor would ever purchase a property without inspecting the foundation of the structure. Do not finalize any real estate transaction without a thorough inspection on the financial foundation of the property.

VIII. THE SHORT SALE CLOSING PROCESS

Every lender and every type of loan has its own specific forms and disclosures that must be completed before a short sale can be finalized. Mortgages in second position also have specific forms and documents required before completion. All of this results in a mountain of paperwork that is best left for your Realtor/ Negotiators. Keep in mind that short sale approvals from lenders are time sensitive. Often times, an incomplete or improperly filled out document will result in the lender requiring the entire package to be resubmitted. This could potentially add weeks or months to your process, and push your seller/homeowner that much closer to foreclosure.

As with every other type of activity or endeavor, there is absolutely no substitute for experience. Repetition leads to perfection. If you are new to the short sale world or are not supremely confident in your ability, do not go it alone. Exercise as much due diligence in the team of professionals you employ to represent you in this process as you did in finding the property itself. Selecting the right Realtor/Negotiator/Legal Discovery Firm will speed up the process, maximize your value and protect your ability to realize the most profit possible on the resale of your asset.

We are here for you. Please contact us with any questions and/ or let us help you successfully buy or sell any residential or commercial real estate. You can contact us at:
Brian@homsaf.com
Catherine@redeemersolutions.com
Toll Free: 800-277-8919

About Brian

After spending ten years in the electronics manufacturing industry as CEO of Epitech and a director of National Manufacturing Technology, Brian Kissinger became a part-time real estate investor in 1999. During the economic collapse of 2008, he assisted a friend with the modification of his defaulted mortgage. He encountered the same convoluted corrupt system that was foreclosing on millions of American families. Because of the succesful IPO of National Manufacturing Technology, Brian was intimately aware of SEC regulations and Securitization Procedures. This experience combined with his knowledge of real estate transaction procedures, conveyances and chain of title assignment legalities, led to the creation of the HoM SaF System and The Aria Management Group.

HoM SaF and The Aria Management Group now exist as full-service asset risk assessment, legal discovery, transaction compliance, auditing and negotiation companies serving real estate investors and the law firms that represent them. With a mission statement of "NO MISTAKE REPEATED, NO DAY UNPREPARED" they are committed to prevention through education. Brian feels that only by exposing the banking and government corruption of the past can citizens protect themselves in the future.

HoM SaF and The Aria Management Group are a consortium of research analysts, paralegals, attorneys, forensic accountants, mortgage professionals, retired SEC and FDIC compliance officers. Their unequaled aggressive and confrontational approach against the world's largest financial institutions delivers the greatest financial savings for their individual clients, while hopefully enacting reforms that will benefit the Nation as a whole.

Contact Info:
Brian@homsaf.com
949-264-2022
www.homsaf.com

About Catherine

Catherine Kaufer has been a Real Estate Broker since 1998 in Northern California. After 14 years of being a Top-Producing Real Estate Broker in the San Francisco Bay Area, in 2008, she noticed that traditional real estate was becoming ineffective. She felt she needed to change with the market and re-evolve as a broker to provide creative ethical solutions for her clients. Being very sensitive and determined to help people resolve their different situations, she invested herself in more comprehensive education, as well as to be coached and associate herself with world-renowned professionals. With this knowledge and application, she was better equipped to provide solutions – from the distressed homeowner to the savvy investor. Her heart is wired to be of service to people, and to direct and guide her clients with solutions that best fit their needs.

Catherine is a full-time, full-service, licensed professional Real Estate Broker who is a member of the National Association of Expert Advisors. Being a Certified Home Selling and Buyer Advisor, she has the skill and knowledge to service her clients with utmost professionalism and results. She works one-on-one with her clients, and has a team of professionals to support her.

Contact Info:
Catherine@redeemersolutions.com
800-277-8919
www.redeemersolutions.com

CPSIA information can be obtained at www.ICGtesting.com
Printed in the USA
BVOW081605280213

314289BV00001B/3/P